Conversations with Your Best Friend

A No-Self Help Book About The Things
Our Parents Didn't Teach Us

Book One

"Written" by
Yoshua

You Enjoy Life Publishing
Denver, CO

"Praise For Yoshua and CWYBF"

"Do not try and read this book, that would be absolutely impossible. Instead, only try to realize the truth...there is no book. In doing so you'll see that it is not the book that gets read, it is yourself."
~The Chosen One

"This was easily one of the most life changing and important books I have ever read in my entire life. Wait, what book are you talking about? Oooh that one... eh, I truly obtained nothing from it."
~Newt Merciful

"When I first read CWYBF I fell asleep within the first 10 pages and upon waking up my shirt changed colors, there was money missing from the counter and I was fully enlightened. It was odd to say the least."
-Levi Ivel

"Yoshua, what you've just written is one of the most insanely idiotic things I have ever read. At no point in your rambling, incoherent musings were you even close to anything that could be considered a rational thought. Everyone in the totality of existence is now dumber for having read it. I award you no stars, and may the Universe have mercy on your soul."
-Milly Badison

Other Books From Yoshua
Official Intelligent Beings
Intelligent Beings

Conversations With Your Best Friend
by Yoshua Greenfield

Published by You Enjoy Life Publishing, Denver Co

International Standard Book Number :
978-0-578-63994-9

Printed in the United States of America

Cover Designed by
TKS Lowskill

Edited By
Anna Wegner

This book was written for, and is dedicated to, YOU.

What You May Find Inside These Pages

Disclaimer:

The author of this book does not make any claims to having any sort of healing abilities or powers, neither of the medical, magical nor supernatural kind, not even of the Harry Potter or Matrix kind (though, I mean, come on, how cool would that be?). Any growth, change, insight, healing or ability to dodge bullets and cast spells that you perceive or acquire is solely caused, experienced, or felt by you—be-it your mind, your physical being, your consciousness, or what have you. The author of the following pages does not have any mind in the matter, and knows, at best, nothing at all. This book is made up of no more than words. Thank you for being here, and, uh, oh, please be sure to silence any devices that may falsely alarm or incorrectly awaken you on this journey.

Before We Begin

Let's Play a Game

In grade school I possessed a very poor vocabulary and my grammar skills sucked at best. Paul, a brown haired, 5'9, fairly athletic built student that looked not unlike a wise owl, that I went to grade school with, seemed to be rather smart—he knew the definition and meaning of just about every word in the dictionary and I always envied him for it. In fact, he knew words so well he often raised his hand in class to correct our teacher for her misuse and misspelling of specific words. Needless to say she didn't like that very much but the other classmates got a kick out of it (which only infuriated her more).

Since my vocabulary was rather arrested in the most basic of ways, I always felt inferior to many of the kids in my class, especially Paul. I couldn't speak nearly as eloquently (a "big" word I wouldn't have dared use back then, oh no) as many of the students seemed to be able to, and rather quickly I decided I must be dumb and would never amount to much of anything as far as general intelligence goes.

I held on to the valuation of "dumb" that I had branded in hot coals on the inside of my mind for a large portion of my life. This label clouded most of the things that I believed and thought about myself, lowering my self-esteem to a shriveled up raisin, and not even the golden kind, the crappy kind you find in a cheap gas station bag of trail mix.

To my great misfortune, I labelled myself in a category that kept me feeling small in almost every situation I wound up in. On top of that I was diagnosed with A.D.H.D and placed on medication for having a "learning disability," which only added to my ever growing list of reasons I felt flat

8

out stupid. My learning was disabled? What in the actual fuck does that even mean? Well, you can imagine what I made it mean. What's more, had I known at the time that all words, and thus their meanings, were made up, and that most people I knew were only playing pretend in life, I may have felt entirely different. But alas, we have one of the great riddles of life.

When I first came to the staggering realization that all words were made up, as you may have yourself, or may be discovering at this very moment (or may be saying, "uh, duh captain obvious" to), I was dumbfounded, perplexed, confused and yet somewhat relieved all at the same time. This profound (or so I thought at the time) discovery didn't come so simple to me, but when it did, I would never read a single thing quite the same again. As I began to see, it wasn't so much the words in and of themselves that were the problem, but rather the way I used them to create a story where I would constantly tell myself about how I was dumb, and thus less than, for not knowing most of them. I held on to that belief for damn near 20 years and boy did that mess me up.

Reading and writing were extremely arduous tasks for me in school. I hardly read a single book until the age of 19 when I was over a year into college. While I did "technically" read before this moment, I strongly despised reading, always thought movies were way better, and could never make it through an entire book, let alone a chapter or page without drifting into a daydream, re-reading sentence after sentence with almost no retention. I relied on spark notes and summaries to get through grade school, and never found myself immersed in a single collection of words, always dreading summer reading like the plague.

One day, to my surprise, that all changed. I fell into a deep love affair with books after a college English class my sophomore year where I was assigned to read 1984 by George Orwell. I didn't finish the book at the time, though I have gone back and re-read it twice as it is so good, but it was my first glimpse of the power and magic of the written word. After that I decided to try and read a book for fun and picked up the Da Vinci Code, which I devoured in a few days, followed by the 4th Harry Potter book, Goblet of Fire, also devoured in lieu of studying for a final, and the rest was history.

The more I fell deeply in love with books, the more I yearned to understand those "big" and "impressive" words that always made me feel so small. When my love for reading finally did come to fruition I couldn't get enough. I was turning into a book junkie needing a continual fix of the good stuff, and found myself lost in books for days at a time.

To make sure I was getting the most out of my experience, I kept a dictionary close by to decipher all of the great mysterious words that always plagued me into inferiority in my earlier years. My dictionary may have been of the electronic kind on my phone, but it seemed to grant me limitless access to a whole new world of words and wonder. It wouldn't be until a few years into my journey, as reading and then writing found a permanent place deep within my heart, that I would discover something so obvious yet elusive that it would rock my world forever.

And so I ask, would you like to play a game? The game is simple, and the rules will reveal themselves as you play the game. Yes? Okay, here goes.

To start, pick a word, a verb or an adjective will work well, that you have always admired, appreciated, or had an interest in. Something that you are fairly certain you know the definition of, but if you were asked to confirm the "text book meaning," you might have to look it up. Heck it could be the word "admire," in fact, I'll use that one. Once you've got your word, look up the definition of that word, selecting the definition that suits you best (if there are multiple ones) and read it out loud.

Admire:
Regard with respect or warm approval.

Upon reading this definition I can think of what I know of the word admire and come to the conclusion that I agree with what I have read and move on with my life. Simple enough? But wait, why are we here, and what is this game all about?

The game that I started playing with myself, the game that would ultimately unravel a key mystery about words for me, came when I realized I didn't know what some of the words in the definition of the very words I was looking up meant, thus having to also look them up. When I look at the above definition, two words that stand out are "respect" and "approval". And so let's see what happens if I dig into those words as well.

Approve:
Officially agree to or accept as satisfactory.

Seems harmless enough. If I approve of something, it makes sense that I would agree or accept that thing.

But what about respect?

Respect
A feeling of deep admiration for someone or something elicited by their abilities, qualities, or achievements.

Ah ha! If part of the definition for admire is to "regard with respect" and part of the definition of respect is "a feeling of deep admiration," what the heck does that tell us? The conclusion that shifted the entire world of words for me in that very instance became ever so clear. As I briefly mentioned earlier; all words are made up, but there is more to the story than that. 'Meaning' simply rests on the meaning of other words, there is no one word that explains another without another explaining it. It goes round and round in one big circle.

And that was the game I started to play—think of a word, look up the definition of that word, and keep searching the words within the definition until you end up back where you started.

What was once so confusing became utterly and plainly clear; sure it may be obvious that language and words are made up, but the piece that was missing was this—we create our own meaning insomuch as we use language to define meaning. It's not that words are not lovely. I appreciate language, it has a lot of value in many ways, but language as an attempt to explain and communicate how we feel, what we believe, what our needs are, and what the heck is really going on in this wild world, is not always the most reliable means of communication and is often misinterpreted.

*To further this concept I will include a variety of "textbook" definitions to common words throughout these pages as a starting point for you to unravel their very nature.

Without the right key for the lock, it's obvious that we can't open the door we are trying to go through, but when it comes to understanding the world around us and getting a clear grasp on information, it's not always so obvious. What if the information we were given was wrong? What if everything we were taught was based on miscommunicated definitions and beliefs? Chances are if you are here than you've had a similar feeling, that something isn't quite right about the life you are living and the way in which you were taught to live in the world around you just doesn't add up.

Imagine for a moment that some of your most precious beliefs, some of the very basic ideas, ideals and morals that you've lived your life by, were complete and utter lies. Maybe these thoughts came from you, or perhaps you learned them elsewhere, things such as; take a safe career path, God is judging you, the world is a scary place, your dreams are unreasonable, every man for himself, they're all going to laugh at you, fear "the man," the list goes on and on. Most people spend their entire lives believing things and making choices that they think are of their own volition when in truth they are simply programmed ideas from past fears and judgments.

I'm not saying this to challenge you on your beliefs, nor do I have an interest in having a pissing match to see who can dominate the conversation with their impressive facts and thoughts on the matter. But I do bring this up for a very specific reason.

If you have strong beliefs, thoughts and ideas that seem to make sense to you, then great, do as you please with them. I'm not here to stroke the ego, to convince you of anything, only to get you to start to look at the parts of YOU that don't feel so good. Just as a doctor might diagnose and attempt to cure a physical ailment or sickness you are experiencing, they wouldn't first look at the parts of you that felt good and search for a cure. Rather, they'd most likely go right to the heart of the problem and work backwards, or forwards, from there.

Ideas and opinions are the dominant life-force of our planet. Opinions toppled on thoughts buried by beliefs compounded by ideas. A human here and there believing that what they have to say is right and often times fighting for what they are so sure they know to be true. But what happens when suddenly you start to see the cracks, start to see that what you were told to believe might not be so true? It's easy to hold on to our beliefs, to cling to them like a safety raft in a shit storm of doubt, but as you may have come to see, our beliefs keep us feeling safe—until they don't.

Conversations With Your Best Friend isn't a book about philosophy, dogma, or religion, nor is it a toolbox of practices for you to follow rigorously. This book is not to be used as a definitive set of rules for a specific way of being, but rather to unravel YOUR way of being. To pull on that loose thread dangling from the depths of your metaphorical (or so very "real" depending on what you believe) soul.

When I took a moment to pause the distractions and dig into my life, I couldn't stop myself from pulling the tiny little thread piercing its head out from underneath my entire being. Like the layers of an onion, when you peel back each layer, you only find another layer, until there is no more onion.

When you take a moment to look honestly into your life, what string is loose, what part of you needs to unravel in order to unveil who you truly are? When I started pulling, I couldn't stop. Sure I tried many times, even tried to cut off the piece that was hanging out, just as I have on many pieces of clothing, but at the end of the day I knew it was already coming undone, that all that held up my belief system was a complex interwoven structure of varying design, built on fear, meant to make me believe I was standing on solid ground.

It is that tiny little thread sticking out that seems so small and insignificant at first, but is the beginning of the entire makeup of our identity, and the moment we see it and start to tug, the bigger the end we are pulling on gets, until we have no defined structure left. Just an undefined piece of string ready to be churned into something new.

Once you see the false reality that makes up you it can be quite challenging to stop seeing it. From my experience, until you've gotten to the core of who you really are, you'll always be moving forward, discovering something new, with each dissolving layer. Chances are, if you are here reading this, then you already know what I am talking about.

Have you ever had a piece of jewelry, rope, or heck a guitar chord, that seemed so tangled that it would be almost impossible to unravel? As a kid girls would always bring their tangled necklaces to me because they knew I loved untangling knots. Each time, without fail, I would untangle what once seemed like a lost mess, and make it whole again. Every time, no matter how complex, hopeless or out of whack a chain, bracelet, or necklace was, I would always come to find that after some dedicated patience at the beginning, it would always hit a point where everything would easily unfold.

You see, no matter how complex your life seems to be, at the end of the day it isn't all that much different from that chain, or rope, or long thin thread, a constructed facade with a most basic nature. I'm still fascinated with my clothing in knowing that no matter how solid or unified any one piece seems to be, when I look close enough, each pair of pants, shirt or jacket is constructed of something so simple and rudimentary, a long thin piece of fabric, woven in a way that gives it the appearance that it is more than it seems, that it is solid when in fact it is formless.

And so it is this book's only design to unravel your seemingly solid structure to aid in showing you what your original thread really looks like. You can think of it like a sort of tearing down of your house, destroying, piece by piece, the building blocks of your life that were built on a weak foundation so you can build up a new one by the universe's perfect design, not the fears and past conditions of others who didn't know any better.

We are complex beings, there is no question about that, but it is through the guiding light of truth, our ability to release control, and a thirst for stopping at nothing until we've seen what is real, that we can unlock the infinitely absurd puzzle that is our supposed "self".

Once I cleared out what didn't serve me anymore (and damn if it ever did), I started to see a clear picture of what life actually was. Not one where we get stuck in a system, told that we can't do things, aren't good enough, or that we need to take certain pills for the rest of our lives if we want any chance at being "normal," but an entirely different paradigm all together.

And from there I was able to see clearly that none of my beliefs, however convincing, were true, and that I had been living as a false representation of myself, not in divine universal alignment with all that is.

If I hadn't taken the journey from that world to the one I now reside in, where life makes perfect sense, I wouldn't be writing about it, maybe only guessing, but I've lived it all first hand— changed my condition from fear to trust, rid myself of the A.D.H.D label, the depression figured out, healed my mind and body from various ailments and sickness without the things I was told I needed, faced my greatest fears, and discovered who I actually was (which, lucky me, was really nothing at all).

At the end of the day, I am no more than a reflection of you, someone that has been where you are, that has taken a good hard look at life and made sense of what previously seemed senseless. When I stripped away the facade, let go of the ego, detached from the false character I once spent so much energy trying to hold up, I was left only with truth and my direct connection to everything.

Consider me a friend that is simply here to show you what is possible when you live beyond the false veil of fear and exist in truth.

And so as we begin, I ask you to take a moment to consider—what do you know, beyond a shadow of doubt, to be true?

(Most of the stories, people, and details henceforth have been slightly altered to hide the identity of certain individuals.)

One
On Self-Help Stuff

Greetings,
You can call me Yoshua.

How are you doing today? Good? Great? Fantastic? Okay? Or terrible? Awful? No good? However you feel is just fine, it's all right, in fact it always has been and always will be and I'm glad to have you here in any form, so please come as you are.

I write these pages as a sort of mental travel guide, or living roadmap for you, giving you a tour of a different sort of life that I've come to understand and make sense of through my experiences with it. And though I've done what I can to share about these things as clearly as possible, regardless of what I write, there is only so much I can do before you filter these words through your own lens and create whatever meaning best suits you in that moment—but more on that later.

One of the most enjoyable books that I have ever read was also one of the shortest—a tiny book, maybe 20 pages or so by RHJ called, "It Works: The Famous Little Red Book That Makes Your Dreams Come True!". What I appreciated about it was how concise it was, there was no fat and fluff, it got straight to the point. After devouring the entire thing in less than 30 minutes or so I was able to continue on with my life, applying what I had learned in a clear and simple manner.

What really resonated with me when I read it wasn't the fact that the information was earth shattering, though it did make some interesting points about how to better your condition in life, but was that it was short and didn't beat around the bush. Around the time I read it, I was starting to get tired of the myriad of personal development books popping up out of nowhere that often droned on and on about the latest new trendy way to help the self.

What I often found was I would be suggested a book by a friend or acquaintance, or sent one by my mom (after all, nothing quite beats a surprise gift like a "you need help" book in the mail from your mom, thanks mom!), and while at times I found the first few chapters and the writer's perspective interesting, after about 50 pages or so it often felt like the book was saying the same thing over and over again, using different stories, quotes, and anecdotes to arduously lengthen a point I had already grasped and was ready to apply.

That is not to say that it has been a problem with all of the personal development, spiritual, and self-help books I've read, there are some that have certainly kept my attention and been helpful through and through. But the more I searched for answers to life's great questions, the more I realized I wasn't interested in length. I have a serious craving for the good stuff, the juicy and tender meat and bones dripping with delicious knowledge and indulgent insight of just the right portion.

Reinforcing a book with stories, facts and studies isn't a problem in and of itself, but at some point the more knowledge we acquire can end up being a distraction from actually applying the information, especially if we get too wrapped up in the words and the person writing them.

I wasn't sure why this phenomenon of lengthy and catchy self-help books was so common until I started speaking to publishers about some book ideas I had come up with. Suddenly it became evident, while the short 30 or so page book I read was an exception to the rule, generally a book had to be a certain length and have a certain modernized twist to be able to market it. It wasn't that the information, or writers point necessarily got more clear and profound throughout the book, maybe it did, maybe it didn't, but that the book had to seem filled with so much good and plenty wisdom to warrant someone buying it instead of simply reading a short article in a magazine or on a news site.

I get that, I really do, business is business, but I also don't care much about what sells and am far more interested in the quality of the content I am digesting than the length. When it comes to life and growth related work, there isn't really that much to say that can't be said in under 50 or so pages if I would have to guess. But people like to read things, as I do, and I figured instead of cutting the book too short and guessing what may or may not resonate with you, I thought it best to include a variety of musings on different facets of life and how they relate to the basic concept of taking a good hard look at yourself.

Which is really what this book is designed to do—assist you in unraveling the confused mess of life that you may have found yourself in, a side effect of being born in a fear-based world, in order to discover something much more interesting waiting for you on the other side. And while there is plenty to read amongst these pages, I suggest that rather than continue to read on and on, if you find that something resonates, consider putting the book down for a bit and seeing how it applies to your life.

Treat each section as its own mini adventure, each chapter offering you something to try on and experience from your own accord. Regardless of how you read this book (chronologically or cherry picking chapters that call to you), I would suggest reading the first 6 chapters in order and then doing as you please. What I have to share doesn't take all that much time to express and is best when it is first experienced, considered and applied before moving on.

I could beat around the bush here and ease into the conversations we are about to have together, but these conversations are not for the casual seeker admiring life on the sidelines, they are really about digging into your life with a battle-axe, incinerating all that arises from fear and exploring the most fundamental truth that we all have to face in life, so I'd rather turn anyone away right off the bat that doesn't, and will not, resonate with what I have to share in this book.

The very least I can do is save you some time and wish you the best on your journey if it ain't this one. But if you do resonate with what you read and feel called to join me on this journey, what lies ahead just might lead you to discovering who YOU really are, or something like that... Sound fun? Scary? Exciting? Feel like you need to puke? Good. All feelings are welcome here.

You see, the path towards enlightenment, awakening, or whatever you want to call it, is not an easy path, but it is a path indeed and one that isn't so simple to get off once you get on, so you might as well buckle up! It is certainly not for everyone and sometimes it can feel easier to try and stay asleep and "fit in," but if truth comes knocking at your door, as it did for Neo when Morpheus revealed to him what he had already been suspecting all along (Cue Keanu's line; "The Matrix"), then I do trust that this book may be a guiding force on this new adventure you are seeking (or being hurled into head first at 1000 miles an hour whether you like it or not).

Woah woah woah, back up a second, did he just throw the "enlightenment" word out there? Really?
Why yes, I did.

It is, for sure, one of those heavy handed words, a word that has been shrouded in mystery and confusion and perplexed even the most accredited thinkers of our time, trust me, I know. But it is also, as I have come to see, and as Jed Mckenna often says, "That which cannot be simpler."

Our preconceived notion that enlightenment is for the few, that truth-realization and waking up from the dream comes only after painstaking years of studying under the finest and most elevated gurus that have been showered in infinite bliss and exotic sounding flowers may hold some value, but the only value I see it holding is to remind us that we must not be distracted by shiny things and must not put others on a pedestal, but rather see that we only need truth to be our guide. The Buddha wasn't the Buddha because he was some sort of God or deity living on earth, but simply a man who went out into the world, took a good hard look at reality, saw the truth of what was really going on, and started to do something about it.

Okay sure, as the tale tells us he was the son of royalty and destined to be this and that, but labels and fables aside, he was no different from you and I (whether he actually existed or not, much like you and I). And though this book is not about Buddhism, realizing that what he attained is available to anyone willing to take an honest look at themselves is a good way to see what is truly possible.

While we all have varied backgrounds, opportunities, and skills in this life, what he had to offer was for anyone, both rich and poor, educated and uneducated, everyone. No matter who you are, what you've done with your time, what you look like, or where you came from, at the most basic level we are all the same and thus have the ability to discover who we really are if we are willing to look.

And that is the basis of where this book begins—the information henceforth isn't for the few "lucky ones," but for anyone willing to try it on. I'm not here to convince you of anything, I'm no politician or sage, no guru or wise master, no elevating being or mystic, no P.H.D or A.D.H.D (even if that last one was a box I was placed in to at a young age), and if you think I am, even in the slightest bit, you are likely already headed in the wrong direction. If you see me as someone above you that has something that you can't attain, you'll only miss the entire point and key to unlock the mystery that is your life. Sure I've learned some things, I've had a good amount of success in the "real" world, but that was all really just a side effect or bonus of what we are here to explore together.

If you are reading this book and have made it this far,

chances are that you do have that burning desire in your soul, that itch that you can't stop scratching, that band aid that you can't help but tear off, doing whatever you must to get to the bottom of whatever the hell is really going on in this crazy world—and I've got nothing against crazy (what's life without a little wackiness from time to time?).

Whether you feel alone in this quest or not, I am here to remind you that you are not alone. By being in the process of digging deeper and deeper into the makeup of you, life will start to make more sense as you uncover more and more about who you really are, or rather are not.

As the Buddha has expressed in one way or another, "I am not here to convince you of anything on blind faith, but I come with an open hand so you can try it on and see for yourself." There are no hidden tricks, no shortcuts or "get enlightened and break free of delusion and fear in 5 easy step schemes," and there certainly aren't any pre-packaged boxes of microwavable truth-realization noodles on the market (that provide you with anything other than the taste of cardboard shit in your mouth, and damned if I don't know, maybe that's the secret!).

No matter what marketing may try and convince us of, telling us that we can have our awakening cake and eat our ego too, which often only serves to build up the false narrative even more, the journey only comes from the honest seeker, the one who is willing, or can't help but, to dig deep into their fears, beliefs and judgments and see what they are really made of when the fire burns all false beliefs to the ground.

I'm trying to find the words to tell you,
But something always comes out wrong.
I may never fail you, but I'll keep hanging on.
The fire burns you bright.
The fire burns you bright.

I may never tell you, I may not come home.
Cause I've got nothing for you, If nothing's right and wrong.

The fire burns you bright.
The fire burns you bright.
Fire burns. Illusion burns.

-You and The Everybody Band, lyrics from "Fire Burns"

I should also add in these early pages that while I will briefly chat about some of the more popular topics you may find in self-help, spiritual, and personal development books—things like love, intention, gratitude, manifestation, flow, and all of that jazz—I'm less interested in giving you more tools to build you up, and more interested in arming you with weapons to tear the false you down. And the reason, though seemingly odd at first, is really quite simple.

Bringing in more love into your life, more compassion, more ways of manifesting and attracting what you want, more practices of gratitude and what have you, though they all have value in their own right and can be glorious things to cultivate, they can often be counter intuitive and even distracting in many cases. These delightful feelings and gifts that you most likely want to have more of can often be the very thing keeping you stuck, keeping you in a constant state of judgment for who you currently are and who you need to be. Just more false self-talk if you ask me. Rather, I find it's best to focus on slaying your falsehood first, and then naturally, almost as if it were a side effect, you just might start to feel more love, gratitude, flow and what have you without much effort at all.

There is a lot of great, wonderful, elevated, and insightful information out there, much of which I'm sure you've read or heard about —be it in a spiritual book, a lecture on mindfulness or an Instagram post with someone sitting peacefully in half lotus meditating on a private beach in Bali, that may have had or will have a big impact on your life. But I'm not here to fill your head with more knowledge—I'm sure you've already got plenty of that—I'm only here to help you burn and decimate the information inside of you that no longer serves you, that causes an interference, that distracts you from really living the truth of who you are, that takes you away from the alignment you are seeking, all so you can empty your cup and begin anew.

You can quote Rumi all day, but if you haven't lived in the truth of what he says, what good is it really other than to impress some friends at a party? I mean it sounds fun, it might even be pretty convincing, but what might you be covering up or hiding behind?

"It is easy for me to put on a show and be cocky, and be flooded with a cocky feeling; and then feel like pretty cool and all that... or I can make all kinds of phony things, you see what I mean? Blinded by it. Or I can show you some really fancy movement. But, to express oneself honestly, not lying to oneself... now that, my friend, is very hard to do." - Bruce Lee

I'm not interested in impressing anyone, or convincing

anyone that I have a strong opinion one way or another, because I don't. Holding on to, and fighting for, my opinions hasn't gotten me anywhere in the grand scheme of things. Everyone has an opinion about one thing or another, but the path to breaking free of delusion requires letting go of beliefs, not strengthening them.

Everyone has something to say because that's what you do in life right? Sit around talking about what you believe, defending your point, fighting those that don't see eye to eye with you. But for what? To be right? To feel good about yourself? To show off? It works in moments and you might even feel pretty good about schooling someone who didn't know any better, but does it ever really last or amount to much of anything?

Why not point the finger back at yourself, why not look at who you really are before going around trying to convince everyone else that they don't know who they are? That's what I did and I had a hell of a time doing it. I suppose in part that is why I felt called to write this book whether anyone reads it or not.

Praise, accolades and awards interest me as much as a swift round-house kick to the genitals. Accolades are not why I write, nor is fame, or anything of a similar nature. I write because I feel called to write, not through forcing myself to do it, but by allowing it to flow through naturally. I think of what it was like when I was going through this process, how I felt alone and wished I had more direction and a reflecting light to remind me I was headed in the right direction, and so I write simply to offer you some guiding thoughts and clarity along your journey.

In my own process of coming to terms with what was happening to me as I woke up, I found that once I got out of the way, once I let go of the character that I thought I was to see what was beyond the mask, that something else started to come through that was far beyond what I could have ever imagined. Not having anyone to turn to made it that much more confusing at first, but as I started to make sense of it all, everything started to come into alignment and I found myself in a world of infinite possibilities.

So fear not, or have as much fear as you need to work up the courage to soldier on, for you may be lost and confused now, but as your reality shifts from confusion to clarity, life just might get a heck of a lot more interesting.

Two

Conversations with Your Best Friend

Friend:

A person with whom one has a bond of mutual affection.

Bond:

Establish a relationship or link with someone based on shared feelings, interests, or experiences.

Affection:

A gentle feeling of fondness or liking.

I can't tell you how many times I've heard someone say some variation of, "You know, you really remind me of my best friend from back home," or, "Have we met? You seem so familiar." For many years I was really put off by the sentiment, annoyed even. It made me feel generic. I had always tried to be a unique individual and hearing that I was like so many others was quite frustrating. I would always politely gesture something to them in the vein of, "That's nice," but deep down I was cringing and questioning my own individuality.

After hearing many similar sentiments for a number of years, and starting to dig into the statement whenever I heard it, asking more and more questions about why they felt this way, it finally started to make sense. It wasn't so much that I was like their friend back home in the ways that I felt made me unique and different, or as though their friend had similar hobbies and interests to me, or looked like me or anything of that sort—it was really just a relatedness, a feeling of comfort, of ease, someone they could talk to without feeling judged, almost like a feeling of home.

The first real sense of the type of friend that I could be for someone traced back to my high school days. One of my best friends at the time, Michael, may have been my size at 5'7 and had a similar brown hair color as I did, but he was far more athletic than I was and was one of our school's star football players, whereas I mostly played the bench and in game comic relief when the going got tough. Michael was popular, charming, friendly, extremely likable, and everyone wanted to speak with him about last night's game whenever we walked down the halls. Meanwhile I just wanted to get the heck to class and not be seen.

One day we were having a conversation when suddenly he asked me something that I would have never expected to hear in a million years. "Josh," he said, "do you ever wonder if you're gay? I mean, I'm not saying that I am, but how would you know if you were?"

"Well, no," I said. "I mean, I have thought about it, but no I don't think I am (more on that later), but I'm not really sure how I would know, I suppose it's just a feeling. Why do you ask?"

"I don't know, it's just that I sometimes wonder, how would you even know something like that? How do people discover that about themselves? Do you think it would be obvious?"

At first it caught me off guard, not in a judgmental way, I just never had someone ask me such a question before, especially not someone that I knew to be so attracted to girls and that seemed obviously straight. It took me many years to fully grasp why he was asking me this but eventually it became clear that he felt a safeness in talking to me, in asking me a question that he was sure others would ridicule and judge him for, especially with all that machismo and testosterone running around in the locker room. He knew he could be vulnerable with me and ask me some of life's bigger questions because he knew I wouldn't make a big deal out of it. He felt comfortable enough to be honest and open around me and for that I was truly grateful.

In the early years I could never really understand why the star athlete of our school would want to be best friends with me of all people, but it would be conversations like this, and so many more, that would start to make sense of the mystery as I reflected back on all the time we spent together (that and likely the fact that I made a mean bacon egg and cheese on a bagel for breakfast whenever he slept over at my house). Michael was an incredible athlete and was thrown in to that role at a young age, but from what I can gather he also happened to be a really sensitive, thoughtful and complex person and wanted a space to share and make sense of the deeper parts of himself that didn't necessarily fit in with his assumed role in life.

Ultimately I uncovered that it wasn't so much about the specific questions he was asking, but having a space to express various curiosities about all sorts of big questions in life that he didn't think he could share with some of his other peers. As someone who was practically playing sports right out of the womb, Michael was constantly surrounded by a certain type of energy, and while he had a lot of love and support in his life, as a boy growing up in the world of competitive sports, he probably felt closed off from sharing the more sensitive side of himself.

Vulnerability, in the testosterone driven and emotionally shut down world we were in, was sadly often a surefire way to get your ass kicked to the curb and ostracized, star athlete or not.

Whereas Michael's life and identity was practically built brick by brick on the football field, sports for me, though I have played many growing up, were never greatly significant in my life and never defined who I was. I enjoyed them, but I knew I was never going to do anything with my athletic (or lack thereof) abilities. But for Michael they were his life, they were such an integral part of his identity, it's what people talked to him about at parties and in class, it's what he was good at and put most of his energy into. It's a huge part, though not all (as I had come to see), of what defined him.

So when Michael went to college, he was suddenly a small fish in a big pond of other star athletes and eventually stopped playing football. He no longer had that brotherhood that we all shared on and off the field in high school, the friends he had grown up around and felt a deep bond with, and our coaches who believed in him, they were all but gone and with it, most likely what he hadn't realized he really loved about sports.

That is when things started to fall apart for Michael. He played for a few years in college but was no longer the "all-star" of the school and perhaps realized that what he loved about sports was not so much the competition as it was the connection. I can't say for sure, and I don't want to make assumptions, but we had a lot of intense conversations around the subject and I knew how much he struggled with it.

Life post sports went on for Michael. He went through a dark battle with depression and bi-polar, got on medication to help, and eventually, much to our dismay, he took his own life the day before Thanksgiving in 2011. My friends and I were devastated, he was the best and had so much love and support in his life. I remember when my best friend Clay called me after I had just dropped him off at his parents' house on our way home from NYC. "Michael's dead," he said. I was shocked, in disbelief, destroyed, heartbroken, and distraught. When we had spoken a few months before, he admitted to me, and as I would later find out, few others, that he had been on suicide watch after some really dark days. After that he seemed to get better and move past it.

We had great conversations around life, and growth and being honest and open and not taking shit from no one. We laughed, shared stories and I remember being really happy for him and where his life was headed, he seemed so light and clear. But it would be the last conversation we ever had before I got the devastating news that would change my life and all of the people he so deeply loved forever. Which brings me to another big reason why I felt so called to share this book and these stories with you.

Conversations With Your Best Friend was written to assist you in creating clarity and finding truth in your life. I wrote this book, in part inspired by Michael and the incredible human that he was, in the hopes that anyone that may be in a tough or confusing place might be able to make sense of their life and free themselves of the weight of a false identity so the goody good stuff, the real stuff, can shine through. I'm in no way pretending that this book is designed to replace medical and professional advice, to each his own, but I've been through a lot of dark and challenging times in my life and what I share just might resonate with you, even if only to remind you that you are not alone.

In many ways it is a rather simple book that explores the most basic of concepts, in other ways it will likely be very challenging and confronting, who knows maybe even earth shattering (sounds fun right?). Either way, it's up to you to decide what will come of YOU and your life as you digest these words. All I am doing is taking common place concepts, thoughts, ideas, and the things we humans tend to struggle with the most, and shedding some new light on them to guide you through this wild thing we call life.

I have seen that often times the simplest of things often create the most impact, that perhaps we wouldn't have so much hate, crime, violence and war if we only had the basics sorted out, you know the juicy stuff underneath the surface. The more I stop automatically blaming others for the toils and troubles of the world, and start looking at who I really am, while creating a non-judgmental place for others to share who they are in any given moment (as we are all always changing), that my life has truly become clear, fulfilling, rich with new experiences, in flow, and filled with long lasting friendships.

No matter how hard I tried, I couldn't save Michael, and as much as I blamed myself for a long time, it wasn't my responsibility, I could not fully understand what he was going through but with the passing of time it started to make more and more sense as I met so many others in similar situations. In a big way it is in his memory, all that I love about him, and all that he has taught me about the importance of savoring this life by living in my truth that I get the inspiration to write. He may have left this world in physical form, but he is still very much here and I feel his presence often.

I do feel a deep sense of connection to every human on the planet, no matter how different, lost, confused, loving, happy or hateful they may feel. I feel a drive, deep down, to share this information with anyone open or willing to listen, because I have no judgment for anyone, no matter how evil they may seem to be. It doesn't mean I condone or support their actions, but I've been through enough in my life to understand why people do what they do, for better or for worse. I can honestly look back at my life and think of countless times where I could have made one wrong decision or one wrong move and been in a much worse place, heck maybe even in the slammer.

But the first step to truly taking on this book and making a huge shift in your life isn't about opening your heart. It's about dissecting your mind, deepening your focus, plowing into your fears, flushing down the shit-bowl that you've been standing in, and quite frankly, getting the heck out of your own way.

The process of waking up is really about recognizing that your life was built around a dualistic reality, one where there are sides—good and bad, right and wrong—when in truth it's all part of the same thing—beliefs. Rather than getting caught up in ideas and opinions, however interesting they may sound, freeing yourself from the illusion you've been living in is really about dissolving those beliefs so you can actually recognize that you are in fact, and have always been, at one with the universe. Not a character trying to fit in to a seemingly random world, but the totality of all that has and ever will be. It may sound like some "far out" concept, but it's not a concept, it just is the way things are, we need only dissolve that which is not true to see all that is. And you don't really know until you know.

Throughout these pages I'll continue to share pieces of my life that played a huge role in my own awakening to the truth of who I am, selecting moments that I feel might be of some value or relatedness to your own journey, from one traveler to another. But I want to make this clear—do not get caught up in the details of the story, focus only on what you feel and where that might lead you to. I'm not saying that my journey is over, that I'm some high flying Guru floating in a permanent state of zen with no worries for the rest of my life, oh no, this isn't about that, whatever the hell you think that might be about.

I am simply in a state of truth fully realized. I've put in the time, deconstructed my false-self and made perfect sense of a previously seemingly senseless world. So while I may be done seeking truth, fully aware, awake or whatever you want to label it, there are still, and will likely always be things I'd like to do in this world—conversations to be had, books to be written, "fish" to fry, mountains to climb, bowel movements I'll certainly need to take.

Recently after posting a video about loneliness I received an email from someone down on his luck, stuck in a dark and hopeless depression asking for some guidance. When I recorded a piece about his situation, with his blessing, offering some insight on luck and breaking out of his spell, he wrote back, to thank me, and tell me that it bothered him that I also struggled with depression since he thought I was such a wonderful person. He could hardly understand the demons that I too was battling.

It wasn't until a few days later that it really struck me just how much someone with the means to reach a larger audience, be it online, or somewhere else, can easily be seen as having it together, you know, the whole "Guru on the hill looking down at their pupils" scenario. Please make no mistake, I have experienced as much darkness, depression, frustration, loss, confusion and fear as the next person. Sure, the world, and life for that matter makes perfect sense to me.

I am aware of who I am and the things that used to get in my way and have put in the time to burn them down to the ground. I've left one life of confusion for one of clarity. But I still feel pain, I still get sad and down from time to time, I still have moments of total uncertainty and insecurity and everything else that comes with these states, and I'm completely fine with that, because I no longer attach good or bad, which is really just another ego thing that serves me not.

Just because I am awake, doesn't mean I am a robot (or jelly roll, yum) in a permanently programmed state of painless bliss and joy floating in an endless sea of unicorn farts. I still have a body, it still feels all sorts of things and even breaks down from time to time, and I wouldn't have it any other way. Drop me in an ocean of deadly sharks and I will certainly feel fear, but now I know fear for what it is and even welcome it where needed. I've simply taken the right steps in the right direction and am here to show you that there is another way to life, even if all hope seems lost.

You are not alone, not even close, and as abstract as it may sound in this moment, we are all in this thing together, strapped onto this giant mass floating in a universe of everything and yet nothing at all. I write because I have the clarity to do so, these words are not my own, I take no ownership of them, they are not for me to cling to, to attach meaning to, but simply to allow to be, to let them out as clearly as possible, and then you can do whatever the heck with them as you wish.

However you might find this book, whatever things you may agree with, or disagree with, are entirely for you to pursue on your own. These words are not about me, what you feel, what you experience is your own experience. You can either choose to look at these words and see me, trying to understand who I am, what I believe, what I think and feel, whether I am completely full of shit or not and enjoy the smell of my own farts, or you can use the reflection of what I say, and how it makes you feel, to explore your own struggles, confusions and beliefs.

No matter how my words make you feel, I ask that you consider that what you are feeling has little to nothing to do with me. I am completely okay if you disagree with something, or many things, that you read in this book, and in some cases I sure hope that you do. I'm not writing to be agreeable, and have come to see that in many cases the challenges are really the best jumping point for you to be inspired or agitated just enough to unlock something new in your own life. Perhaps my thoughts and ideas, even if seemingly opposing at times, make you more sure of your own, or maybe they make you think outside of yourself and try something new for a change of perspective. Whatever it may be, frankly there is no "me" behind this book.

Warning; by the time you read this, my attachment to these words and stories will have extinguished onto the pages and have fully self destructed.

Let me offer you a little key to make reading this more fluid. A simple way to read and digest this book is as a conversation of sorts (hence the title). Imagine, if you will, that we are sitting and having a chat. "Me" being the words you are reading, and "You" being the thoughts processing, and making sense of those words.

If at any given time you are finding that your brain starts to question things, is racing at a million miles, or starts turning into microwaved goo, I suggest you put the book down, pick up a journal, a notepad or any of your preferred writing devices, and begin writing. What about doesn't really matter, so long as you keep writing, unfiltered, until you get everything racing around in your head out. You can even act as though you are writing to me or someone you trust and care about.

Sometimes it helps to have someone to direct your words towards even if they never read them, and heck you can even send me an email or message if you feel compelled to do so, I'm pretty easy to find via a quick interweb search of You Enjoy Life. As you write, just know that I am not here to judge you for anything you could ever say or think, no matter how absurd or seemingly odd it may be. In fact I am almost positive that anything you might write I've likely thought about or experienced in one way or another. Write, unfiltered, without going back and editing what you wrote until you feel you've gotten it all out, just let it flow. In each of us is the totality of the universe, no topic, idea, thought or experience is off limits. And if it helps you can burn up your words after you've shed them onto the page.

As much as you may like to think that your mind has the capacity to do a lot of serious thinking on its own up there, thoughts often only swirl from one to another (at least from my experience, maybe your brain is more organized). By putting them on the page, to be released, examined, and expelled, we can start to make room for what is to come. Think about it like taking a big ol' mental dump onto the page, if you are swimming around in your own fish bowl of crap you might not realize how murky the water is until you flush the waste down the toilet. Let it out, write, write, write, don't criticize and review what you are writing until it is all out. And once you are done writing, come back here, or heck write some more, or do whatever feels right in the moment. Whatever happens, you just might find some relief and clarity as you expel what serves you no more.

Three
Things Our Parents Didn't Teach Us

Parent:
A father or mother; one who begets or one who gives birth to or nurtures and raises a child; a relative who plays the role of guardian.

This book could have just as easily been named "Things Our Parents Didn't Teach Us," but I didn't want to start off this journey by titling my book with something that might insinuate any blame towards someone, let alone my parents (the subtitle felt far more suitable). And the same goes for anyone I write about in this book. There is no situation, person, place or thing that I hold any blame for. All stories and people mentioned in this book, are people that I have nothing but love and appreciation for. I only share stories with the hope that it may inspire or resonate with you in some way.

There was however a time when I had a lot of blame in my heart, blame that led to frustration, anger, and even hate, but that has all melted away as I unraveled my sweater. Do I still get angry and feel frustration from time to time? Of course I do, but I don't hold on to it any longer than I need to. Like a bottle in my hand, my grip is just tight enough so I know it's there and can be dropped the moment clarity comes in to view. I don't ever blame anyone else for my condition, rather I look in the direction of truth and understanding.

Which brings me back to the title of this chapter. I wanted to start off this section by including the definition of parent for the simple reason that I felt it necessary to start with a baseline for what we generally believe a parent to be. Regardless of what you may have come to believe your parents' purpose is within the context of your life's story, consider that when I say parent, I really speak to the people who ultimately raised you and helped shape who you are in a big way. It would be as simple to say anyone that raises you, either biological or otherwise, but who is to say that there was any one, or two people who had the most influence in raising you in the world?

In my case I have two parents who are still together. My parents raised me with the support of those around them; other relatives, friends, and even some hired help from time to time. However, since I didn't grow up in a rural village in the woods where everyone took care of everyone else, but instead in a very weird 1980's America, as the eldest of three, I spent the bulk of my early childhood under my parents rule. They weren't super strict parents, but they were mine and they raised me the best they could.

Being that as it may, while I am biologically my parents child, and while a good portion of my conditioned responses were directly imprinted from my parents, I also experienced strong influence elsewhere in my life. Regardless of your belief of nature vs nurture—to which I have a few fun ones myself (yay for more beliefs!)—as a child I took in the world around me, learning and growing as I went, doing my best to process all of the seemingly contradictory information I was ingesting. I didn't know it was all made up at the time, which of course only made it all the more confusing the moment I started to dig into who I thought I was.

And so when I speak to the things I "wish" my parents taught me, while it is easy, and in many ways valuable to look directly at my actual parents, I want to make it very clear that I am not only speaking about my parents, but everyone and everything that ultimately helped shape and form me into who I am today. My parents, relatives, teachers, friends, books, video games, movies, just to name a few—all had a very pivotal role in helping me form my identity. I don't hold any blame towards anyone or anything for any "shortcomings" that I may have had in this lifetime, but you can bet your ass there were things that I so truly "wished" I learned growing up and I figured the least I could do was write a book all about the stuff I would have loved to know from the get go.

How can we wish we had something or knew something, without first having it to know that it is something we truly desire? Otherwise we are only projecting the belief and outcome that we place upon seeing another have something and assuming it to be something we would like to have. I'm not here to guess how that works but having direct exposure to guiding factors that made my life make a heck of a lot more sense, there are a lot of things that I wish my parents, teachers and books taught me.

Throughout the course of my life, as I discovered different nuggets of hidden wisdom, I remember so many times being frustrated and even enraged that I was not taught them before, for how easy life would have been! Later on, being on the flip side of that story, I started to see the wonder in not knowing something, in discovering something for myself, as a way to truly know it.

"You shall no longer take things at second or third hand, not look through the eyes of the dead, nor feed on the spectres in books. You shall not look through my eyes either, nor take things from me, you shall listen to all sides and filter them from yourself."
- Walt Whitman from "Song of Myself"

As a guitar player who has taken random lessons here and there but is mostly self-taught, I remember discovering some fundamental things out on my own about the guitar, things I missed because I never learned how to read music, that unlocked a whole new world for me. Sure it would have been great to know them before, but the process of self-discovering something, even if it was common knowledge elsewhere, was wonderful. I started to do little exercises where I would pretend that I invented the guitar, that there was no previous information on it, and I had to discover how to use the instrument as if it were some alien foreign object. Knowledge was great, but my real creativity came when I threw out that knowledge and saw what I could come up with as if I was a pioneer of the guitar.

I started approaching life like this. Sure I would love to learn as much as I could about a subject or interest, lord knows there is enough information on the internet and in books about everything, but I also found it endlessly enjoyable to approach life as an explorer. When we learn something directly through another as a way to mimic what they do we may be able to learn a great deal and draw a lot of good from these interactions, but we also run the risk of falling prey to picking up their bad habits, should they have any (and they most likely do), while boxing ourselves in to their specific teaching style or philosophy.

We also tend to blind ourselves to seeing new things that our teacher may have not seen, thus closing off potentially profound information and insight into the subject matter. After all, information is always changing and it often takes thinking out of the box, or a mistake, to break into something new.

As you continue to read on, while you are undoubtedly going to be filtering the words through your own lens, there is an opportunity to see both old and new concepts in a different light. I am not here to convince you of anything or to share my beliefs with you in the hopes that you see my point of view. All I suggest is that you take a look for yourself, not take the things that I am saying to be truth, nor opinion or even theory. I simply offer you to try them on for yourself and if something resonates, opens up or challenges you, lean in to it and enjoy the ride.

Lego My Ego

The dictionary definition of Ego:
A person's sense of self-esteem or self-importance.

Ego is one of those weighted words that really trips people up, and since it comes up quite a bit in this book, I thought I'd take a moment to clear up something. When I use the word "ego" I am only referring to that in which we think we are. I don't mean ego in a negative way, nor a positive way. Not in the, "He is an egomaniac" or a, "check your ego at the door!" kind of way either. I refer to ego only as the thing in which we think we are; the stories, beliefs, ideas, thoughts and judgments that we have of our existence.

The ego is the part of you that you consider to be yourself, which, for the sake of this book, we can use interchangeably with the false-self. There is nothing wrong with having an ego, your ego can't choose to have no ego either. How could something consciously choose to be nothing?

The ego is the thing that allows us to exist as a human in the world, creating a framework for us to interact with others, and yet it's the first thing that we must examine in order to get to the bottom of this whole "Who the hell am I?" life quest that we are on. You know, basic stuff, just another day at the office...

Four

On Spirituality, Enlightenment and Other Sometimes Silly Stuff

"My eyes are open," said Milo warmly, "and I see exactly what I expect to see. I see a man who is terribly wounded—because he has dared to pass through the fires of truth to the other side, which we have never seen. And then he has come back again—to tell us about the other side."

-Excerpt from "Breakfast of Champions" by Kurt Vonnegut

I didn't grow up in a spiritually inclined household by any stretch of the term. My parents never spoke of meditation, yoga, breath-work, mindfulness, the Buddha or even God. We were "technically" raised religious but it always felt more about the social aspects of sticking together with people of our "kind" than it did the higher power stuff. I wasn't really exposed to any level of spirituality, or outside of my "norm" thinking and perspective as a child (and if anything only as the butt of a joke on tv). That was until my girlfriend in high school suggested that I read a book called "Many Lives, Many Masters".

She explained the premise to me: a true story about a therapist who practices regression hypnosis and one day takes someone back so far in their life that they were able to access past lives and speak with ascended masters and explain ancient information they didn't know in their waking state in tremendous detail. I laughed when I heard this and wrote it off as folklore and silly hippie dippy stuff—even if my friends thought I was a hippie for listening to Phish. I was somewhat of a man, okay boy, of science. I didn't believe in God or a higher power, and though I was slowly becoming obsessed with the Harry Potter series, I was all but sure anything that dealt in the magical, mystical or spiritual world was little more than absurd and purely fantastical for the sake of story and entertainment.

When college rolled around, as the story goes, I started a band and within a few years my life was changing more drastically than I could have imagined. My mind was opening up to new thoughts and ideas, and suddenly a lot of the things that I had written off as impossible and extremely ridiculous, I wasn't so closed off to. When I finally threw out my Adderall after the recognition that I had become a slave to it, realizing that I didn't want to rely on medication to help me focus, I started to look in different directions for mind clarity, focus and mental support.

One day, while in a book store looking for books on music, I wandered into the "self-help" section and, remembering the book my then-previous girlfriend had suggested, found it and bought it, along with a second book of the author's that was all about meditation, complete with bonus CD that included a guided meditation.

The author, Brian Weiss, had devised a helpful and straightforward book to help the reader follow a simple meditation through the help of his soothing voice and some very expansive and spacey synth landscape music. I decided to start myself off easy by reading the meditation book before daring to look into his other book which I secretly feared just a little bit even if I didn't know why. Within a few weeks of listening to this 30-minute meditation I slowly noticed a huge shift in the way I experienced my body the more and more I practiced.

Being diagnosed with A.D.H.D at such a young age, I had come to understand, or at the very least been told to believe, that I could never be still, both in my mind and body. Whether my thoughts were racing from one thing to the next plagued with a million ideas before even considering how to pursue one of them, or my body was bouncing up and down the room, arms twitching, head tweaking, I could hardly find a moment of peace and calm.

I even remember the day I was tested to get diagnosed with A.D.D. "Yes, based on the tests today it is clear you have A.D..." She said, cutting herself off mid-sentence as I impulsively tweaked my leg and spilled her coffee all over the test papers. "Scratch that, A.D.H.D". Getting me to sit still of my own accord was like attempting to get a hummingbird to stop flapping its wings.

So when it came to meditation, as I would lie on my back and hear the words softly whispered into my ear that went something like, "Relax your body, gently breathing in while listening to my calming voice," I struggled greatly to not constantly twitch and move around. The first few weeks were frustrating, listening to relaxing music, yet feeling anything but relaxed and calm, I nearly gave up the whole thing entirely. But then I started to find that if I tried to meditate after dancing for a bit, having released a lot of my anxious energy, I was able to sit still for longer and longer periods of time.

Before I knew it, I could make it the entire way through the meditation without moving a single muscle in my body, and honestly without falling asleep, as I often did early on. I suddenly started to feel a tremendous amount of calm that I had never experienced before, which opened me up to a new way of seeing myself and gave me the push that I needed to start reading his other book. I had resistance to it for a number of reasons, but I think the main reason was that deep down I was worried what would happen if I liked it. What would I tell my friends and family, what would they think of me? Gosh, I was already weird enough for them.

In the book, the author Brian Weiss, licensed psychiatrist and hypnotherapist (oooh fancy), explains how he had been keeping a secret he discovered with a patient of his for years and years out of fear of being abandoned, ostracized and ridiculed by his colleagues and peers. He goes on to share the tale of how he uncovered something so profound yet so out of his range of understanding that he hid it from the world until one day he felt he could hide it no more for the simple fact that it could change so many people's lives. Okay, I'm listening, I thought. When I started reading his first book, which mostly focused around the first experience he had with a client of his, I suddenly became engrossed in his story. I was completely obsessed and wanting to read more and more.

As his story goes, it all happened while he was taking one of his clients through a hypnosis session, one where he was using regression hypnosis to bring her back to when she was a child. It's a somewhat common practice for therapists to take their patient into a hypnotic state and help them tap into their childhood to remember repressed experiences, things that may be shaping and coloring their current life.

By uncovering something traumatic, the therapist can help their patient clear the experience, or at least talk through it and help them find some healing. I was new to this stuff but I was also taking some basic psychology classes and what I gathered seemed to make enough sense. As I read on I found it fascinating to learn how the patient would, in their hypnotized state, start to speak as though they were a child, like they could access their memories so clearly that they were embodying that part of themselves.

But then things started to get really weird and wild when, during a session, something drastically shifted, and suddenly the patient wasn't embodying their childhood self, but was speaking as though they were in a past life. Brian went on to express that during the sessions, as he took her further and further back into her past, the patient was able to explain things from a past life in exquisite detail. I think it was in Egypt or somewhere in ancient times, hundreds if not thousands of years ago, things that she could not have known in a waking state. The patient wasn't any kind of expert in Egyptian history, and the details were so vivid that Brian could hardly believe it. There was no way that she could have known these things based on her life's experiences and after a number of sessions he knew there had to be some truth to her regression experience.

As the sessions went on, not only was he able to take her back to past lives and help her tap into powerful experiences, discovering how she died in past lives, such as an incident of drowning, which explained her current fear of water, but he then shared that, in between the state of her going from this life to a past life, that these so called "masters" would speak through her, and offer up profound wisdom about life. The masters, speaking through the client, would talk in a very different voice and speak of prophetic wisdom about life, as though they were speaking directly to Brian, sharing profound insights for him to record.

At this point I was fully hooked, regardless of how weird and silly it may have seemed to hear something like this at any point in my life, the way the book was written, and the feeling I had when I was reading it, took away almost any doubt that what he was sharing wasn't true. And while I quickly realized that the validity of the stories he was sharing were not something I could see for myself, that it didn't matter so much, and I didn't have to accept them to be true or not. It was at that point my mind was opening to the possibility that things were not quite as they seemed and that it might be good to do some more digging. It wouldn't be for a few years later, when I was newly single, living in Brooklyn, and healing from a breakup, that I would dive back in to spirituality, which seemed to find me whether I was looking or not, and continue on a course that would change my life in ways I had no way of knowing.

The Depressedigator

One day, after less than a year or so of living in Brooklyn NY, pursuing my dream of being a musician with my band and landing a job as a private eye that had me sitting in my car for most of the day, I was walking through union square with a new friend, Casey. She was blonde, slender, southern and charming and, truth be told, I had a bit of a crush on her. As we walked down the sprawling streets amongst the hustle and bustle I hardly noticed that I was being drawn, almost as if from deep within, towards what would later seem to be my destiny.

We started walking at the top of the park on this beautiful day with the sun floating gently above the sky and puffy clouds dispersed here and there. We were around 16th street, heading south towards the subway to hop on the L train. With each pacing step, I noticed a resounding echo, a faint voice of gentle levity, bouncing off the trees, but I could hardly make out the words. As the voice got louder with each passing step, I gazed upon a vast group of hundreds of people from around the world attentively listening to a man that looked to be some sort of monk; bright orange robe, shaved head, calm and gentle demeanor and all smiles, ongoing listeners hanging on his every word.

Slowly we started to piece together the colors, symbols and signs (and by quietly asking someone in the crowd), that the monk was Buddhist and that the event was a celebration and appreciation for Buddhism. I asked Casey if she knew anything about Buddhism and after a few minutes of pondering we both came to the conclusion that neither of us knew a damn thing other than that it seemed to be a rather peaceful sort of religion. I could have simply walked away and forgotten the moment, moved on with my life, but a gentle curiosity started to permeate my being and I couldn't shake it.

Just to back up a little bit and fill you in on an essential piece of this story's puzzle,—at the time I was going through a dark depression that I had never experienced the likes of before. Though I didn't know it until years later, depression and anxiety were two things that followed me around like an invisible plague, pulling me down whenever things got tough. Heartbreak was typically the culprit but to me it seemed perfectly normal to go to these places when life handed me a big old bag of lemons, so I thought little of it... until I started to do some digging.

Here I was, less than a year into living in Brooklyn, pursuing my dream of being a rock star, spending a lot of time in my car thanks to my job as a private investigator, when things started to get a lot more bleak. With all of this time on my hands, sitting around, waiting somewhat patiently in my car, doing what I could to snap a shot of whoever I was investigating for the case that day, I started to write about the things I was feeling and thinking about. I was never a writer growing up, never really kept much of a journal, and though I had started to write songs in college, sharing my feelings on an open piece of paper was something entirely new for me.

A week into being a private eye, just after my girlfriend and I broke up, something shifted for me. I was stuck in my car most of the day, and while the job occasionally would turn into a thrilling action adventure, 75% of the time I was alone with no more than my thoughts. I started to put them down on paper, perhaps a response to an imagined fear of losing my mind and getting lost in my head while "trapped" in a tiny heat box waiting for something exciting to happen.

Before I knew it, I was writing non-stop for hours, pouring my heart out, expressing every thought, emotion and desire that rustled its way out of me and onto the pages. My heart broke open and all I could do was share what I felt--every thought that was racing through my mind. I could hardly contain myself. At first it felt really freeing. I started with all of the thoughts I had been holding onto about my past relationship, what I thought really broke us apart, how I felt about my previous partner, the things I wish I had done better, the things I felt I had done right, and the many more I had certainly done wrong. I was processing my relationship in a way I had never done before.

At first it was my relationship that I was processing, but suddenly it was everything in my life, who I was, my family, the choices I had made, what I felt about certain people and influences in my life, what I thought about the world. As I wove through the pages I started to discover key insights that helped me make sense of my entire life up to that moment

(And if your brain is starting to race it might be a good time to put this book down and do some writing).

And then something strange started to happen. I found myself, before I would dig in to my daily writing session, reviewing the notes I had taken the day before, only to find that what I felt the day before was complete nonsense and I had missed the mark. After reading through what I was so sure was a misstep on my part from the day before, I found myself writing new thoughts, now having felt that I had discovered the answer. What seemed obviously wrong the day before, now, having a new perspective seemed completely right.

How foolish I had been yesterday! You idiot! Whether it was to a great mystery in life, such as why we are here, or something more basic such as what went wrong in my relationship, it didn't matter. Each day, as I wrote, I was sure this new insight was the truth, and that the previous day had been all wrong. Again, you idiot!

The more this pattern went on, the more my life began to shift. At first it was exhilarating, uncovering things about myself and the world that I had never really taken the time to examine and ponder, even if I was mostly stuck in my car for hours at a time often in the blistering heat. But slowly, as I wrote more and more and uncovered new understandings and clarity each day, I found myself sinking deeper and deeper into depression.

One day, as I sat there writing, I came upon a truth, a rather simple yet elusive truth, that hit me like slamming into a brick wall. I explained this in a similar fashion earlier on in the book but as a short refresher; Everything that I was writing, all sentences, words, and phrases, all of it, without exception, was made up. Every language had their own interpretation of words, their own form of communication, and that regardless of how real some words might seem, how innate they might feel, all words were made up by someone. And if words were made up, so were their meanings, however true they felt. Within a matter of days, if not hours, I had unravelled my life and discovered that nothing had any meaning, that it was empty and pointless, that all of life was nothing more than lies.

Shortly after this discovery, while speaking to a dear friend of mine and telling her that I believed in nothing, that all of life was made up, she rebuked me and quoted the famous Abraham Lincoln line, "If you don't stand for something, you'll fall for anything". It may have been helpful in another scenario but I couldn't help but immediately brushed it off, thinking only; *Ha, more words!* How could another sentence of gibberish, another belief, another utterance of complete bullshit—no matter how well respected and admired it was, break me free from this downward spiral?

Things only got considerably worse from there. I started to ponder the end of my life. I felt little drive to do anything much at that point. Some days were fine, I suppose, I lost myself in the music, or found distraction in the city with all of its mesmerizing chaotic energy, but when I was alone, back in that car, I questioned whether I wanted to live anymore. If everything was made up and nothing has any intrinsic meaning, what was the point of living? I pondered this point day after day, over and over again, only to come up short with less than nothing.

I can't say that I ever felt seriously suicidal. I didn't write a letter (more words) or have a plan in place, but I did feel like I didn't want to live anymore and lost nearly all of my drive to succeed and to grow in life. Things continued to get really dark and bleak and I had no one I felt I could talk to help me make any sense of it. All I felt was sadness and isolation. Maybe I didn't want to end my life but if it had ended at any moment I think I would have been okay with that because I had no desire to go on in this state. "What's a life good for anyway if it's all meaningless?" I wondered.

But there I was, days, if not weeks, later, at this Buddhist celebration, with my friend Casey, trying to pretend like everything was okay, not having any clue that it would become one of the most important and world altering days in my life. Though I didn't know it, something deep inside—something big was working to point me in a new direction, to take what I was feeling, and turn it all around, even if I felt no hope at all.

Buddha on the Street

I parted ways with Casey and hopped on the L train to head back home from Union Square. It was a short ride, no more than ten minutes from entering the subway to zipping under a long tunnel underneath the water, ears popping and all, ultimately arriving back in Williamsburg. When I trudged up the subway stairs I began the scenic hipster filled two block walk home on Bedford Avenue from N 7th Street to N 5th, where our loft was located. All along the one way strip of street, throughout the day, there were usually simple foldable tables set up lined with a plethora of books with a microcosm of middle aged patrons standing behind each section ready to exchange their goods for your greens.

The books on this pseudo black market display ranged from the coming of age classics like Catcher in the Rye to cookbooks from around the world, to history (the kind you don't necessarily see in public school), and almost anything else you could imagine. Having very little money at the time, though being an avid reader, I found the affordable street selection a great way to pick up a popular book that I had never found the time to read but was told I ought to.

Skimming through the various collections of writings I stumbled upon a tiny book with a picture of the Buddha on it. It was one of those mini bathroom sized readers that fit easily in the palm of my hand, and seeing as how it was only $3, I jumped at the opportunity to get it— noting that I had, no more than an hour before, mentioned to my friend that I knew nothing about Buddhism but was curious to find out more. Perhaps it was fate, but at the time I didn't believe in much of anything, so I hardly noticed the magnetic pull driving me to take out my wallet (which was all but empty) and hand the man three of the last four dollars I had in there.

When I arrived back home I jumped in bed and began reading, almost as if unconsciously desperate to do anything to break me out of my sunken shallows. As I turned the pages, connecting with each and every word that entered my mind, I suddenly found excitement and joy flooding back into my being. *Where have you been my old friend you elusive bastard!* Suddenly everything I had been writing about over the past months—all of my struggles, confusions and darkness—all made sense. I felt a profound sense of clarity and understanding as I read the words and teachings of the Buddha. The more I read, the more his words seemed to merge with my own thoughts, and I felt a deep and profound connection to all that he was saying.

What I found so "enlightening" about it was the simple tale of a man, not a God or religious deity as I had assumed him to be based on how he was worshiped, but simply a man, one who went into the world, saw how much suffering there was in the world, and dedicated his life to finding truth and a way to abolish suffering in a way that anyone could follow. All of the seemingly negative and heavy thoughts I had been holding on to suddenly made sense. The Buddha had had those same thoughts about nothingness and meaninglessness, but found a way to make sense of them and find freedom and clarity within the same things that had been bringing me into the darkest of dark places only moments before.

From my perspective it was almost as if he felt exactly what I was feeling, but had a positive and purposeful spin on it, and within a manner of minutes, I felt it too. It felt like destiny had driven me to find curiosity in Buddhism, from seeing the demonstration earlier that day, to picking up the book, reading it and thus discovering everything I had missed about the beauty of meaninglessness. Had I had a mentor or powerful figure in my life at the time to send me some guidance, maybe I wouldn't have needed his words, but it was as if he was speaking to me, as if I was him, or one with him, as strange as that sounds--I felt what it was like to experience my Buddha nature.

The next year my life continued to shift drastically. I dove head first into all things Buddhism; buying every book, going to meditations, meeting Buddhists, studying the ancient teachings rigorously, buying a few knick knacks and I even started to teach it (and honestly preach it) to my friends, and really anyone that would listen. I wasn't really sure what to make of it all, but I knew that nothing in my life would ever be the same. Suddenly I was becoming a Buddhist...

How Could I Have Missed Something so Obvious?

Up to that point, aside from music, I hadn't taken anything in my life very seriously. I found certain topics to be interesting, I had a variety of hobbies, I would read a book in this or that, I was also developing a bit of a juggling obsession and consider myself a pretty good three ball freestyle juggler, but not much else lit me up in life. Suddenly, however, there I was, completely enthralled by Buddhism. I spent every free moment I had learning more about his teachings, doing my best to apply them to my own life all while having a direct experience with the benefits whenever I did.

After searching the streets of Bedford for any other Buddhist books I could find, I stumbled upon a book that seemed legit enough (based solely on my judgment of the cover, go figure) called "What the Buddha Taught".

The book had me completely immersed in the Buddha and his story. I learned about the origins of the Buddha and how he was a man born of royalty who had parents that believed he was destined to be a great ruler someday over his people, and gave him every advantage they could to make him do so. And how he, feeling stuck inside the palace as a prince, went outside one day and saw suffering, pain and anguish amongst so many of his people who struggled to get by and survive on hardly anything. Feeling such a deep state of compassion for his people he decided to leave his kingdom against his parents desires, become a recluse and live as an ascetic in hopes of finding out a way to help those that he saw suffering.

Throughout his time, Gautama, his birth name, left his world of riches and power to search for the meaning of life and a way to end suffering for all. There are hundreds upon hundreds of stories about the Buddha, some (if not most) myths and fables that even delve into the supernatural, but what I learned and come to appreciate was this:

The Buddha was just a man, not a God or an Angel, or anything especially supernatural, but a man who went into the world, saw that the world was filled with suffering, and devised a set of guidelines to overcome that suffering. I'm not here to sell Buddhism to you, my only interest at the moment is to give a basic breakdown of Buddhism so you can get enough of a grasp of it to see why it was the first spark that sent me on a new path.

The Buddha, as a man who saw the immense suffering people endured, discovered that the heart of suffering stemmed from the fact that the world is impermanent, ever changing, and that when we try so desperately to hold on to things that are always changing, we suffer. Let's say that you have a job that you love, the perfect career path, working for the best company, with a great boss and good pay. Without fully realizing it, you may hold so much pleasure and joy in the fact that you've got this great job, it makes you feel good, accomplished, secure, and happy. But what happens when suddenly you find out your company has to lay off workers and you are one of the first to go?

Suddenly the job is gone, the security and sense of accomplishment all disappears with it, and so what happens? Most likely you suffer... You get upset, sad, depressed, you may even feel an immense sense of fear, worried that the world has thrown you a giant curveball and that life is only going to get worse. That feeling all stems from attachment, perhaps the attachment to the idea that you need something such as a "high paying job" in order to feel good, be safe, and survive.

It's the same with love. When losing someone we love, or going through a bad breakup, we feel so much pain because we are attached to something that will ultimately, at one point in time, disappear, change or grow into something else. Now, this is only a piece of what the Buddha taught, but it is at the heart of the pain and suffering that we experience. Life is transient and ever changing, no matter how hard we try and hold onto things, they are going to change, so the best we can do is accept the change and move forward—growing with the ever shifting currents of life, instead of fighting against them.

This isn't to say you should shut all of your feelings off (though admittedly, to some dismay, I briefly hit a point where I felt that was the right thing to do), but by having this awareness, you can move through life in a more fluid manner. The Buddha also spoke of mindset, conditioning and a number of other important topics all designed to help anyone break free of suffering.

His information was valuable for all, not just those that were well off, even the poorest people in the world could reap all of the benefits of his teachings. He was not someone who went off of blind faith either. He wasn't approaching people from the perspective of being a holy man or a deity and he didn't want people to believe him, it wasn't about that.

Unlike a closed fist approach to life, with someone telling you to believe something that you can't see on blind faith, which often happens in religion, the Buddha always had an open hand, inviting others to come see for themselves and to try on his teachings to see how they may be helpful when applied to one's own life. His teachings also involved having the right actions, right mindset, and right thoughts, all by examining the things that you do, think and are. By doing this you could align with being in truth, not falsehood, and eventually reach enlightenment and thus freedom, attaining Buddha nature, Nirvana, or whatever you want to call it.

For months on end, I was completely immersed in Buddhism and started exploring new types of meditations and different conditioning exercises. One of the most impactful of these experiences came one day when I was driving home from work in heavy traffic. Every day that I got off at a normal hour I would inevitably run into terrible city traffic, and would become stressed out and frustrated almost immediately. Quickly I would lose my patience and boil with anger, beeping my horn in the endless sea of commuters desperate to get the hell out of their cars and on to whatever thing they so badly needed to get to.

Throughout my life I assumed this was perfectly normal. Not something I looked forward to or enjoyed in any way, but I didn't question the feeling of stress. As I started learning more and more about the Buddhist mindset, I decided to challenge these assumptions and change how I looked at the situation. The following week, on a Monday, the moment I pulled up to traffic I immediately noticed my stress level go up, except this time, after a few minutes, I was aware of what I was feeling, like another piece of me seeing how I reacted. I checked in with my thoughts, took note of the feeling that arose within me, however seemingly negative they were, and started talking about it out loud to myself.

"Okay, I am in traffic," I said. "It's frustrating, I just want to get home, play some music and eat a little food, but I am stuck here only a few miles from home in a stand still. This sucks." Then I started to think about why it sucked and the only conclusion I came up with was that I was delaying something that I knew would bring me pleasure and enjoyment. I then looked around and saw hundreds, if not thousands of other cars all in the same standstill, and suddenly I realized it wasn't just me that was stressed. I imagined my scenario almost as if it was a collective feeling amongst a lot of people and that I wasn't alone in how I felt.

And then I took it a step further and wondered about the people that were really suffering from the traffic. Perhaps the traffic was holding someone up who had a serious meeting to get too that could decide the fate of their year, or maybe even worse, someone was sick and trying to rush to the hospital, or that someone just got in a bad accident and was in a far worse situation than I. The more I thought about different possibilities, the more I realized that the stress I felt wasn't really justified, instead it was a conditioned response that wasn't necessary and had zero benefit.

Up until that point in my life I never really understood conditioning, didn't even know what it meant, never truly got how it crafted who I was and how I was in the world, but suddenly I could see who I had become and what I could do to change it. For the rest of the week, every time I pulled up to traffic, I did my best to be aware of the feelings arising within me. At first it was challenging, and I felt the stress and frustration I had before, but with each passing day, it slowly became easier to deal with. I found that I could overcome the stress faster simply by being aware of what I felt and why I felt it. My experiment started on a Monday, and by Friday, the worst of all traffic days, I distinctly remember pulling up to traffic and not feeling anything but peace and calm. It was glorious to say the least.

After spending a solid four to five months practicing, studying and learning everything I could about Buddhism, my life was shifting in profound ways. The conversations I had with people were more honest and I was finding ways to overcome stressful situations and break bad thought patterns. Although I enjoyed sharing about Buddhism, I started to feel isolated in the fact that I didn't know anyone else who practiced Buddhism. I was attempting to teach people that I felt could deeply value the teachings, and I wanted to see what it would be like to meet others out there in the Buddhist world, so I signed up for my first Buddhist meditation class in Union Square--of all places.

When I walked up the two-story walkup a few days later, I entered into a small, but long room with about 15 white foldable chairs set up, some colorful candles burning, a small shrine with a gold statue of the Buddha on it and a picture of an old man who appeared to be a monk or sage of some sort. At the door I was greeted by a friendly and heavyset woman in her mid-30s wearing red robes with a pleasant smile on her face. I signed in, paid my $20 donation and took a seat.

As the class started I noticed there were only 4-5 people sitting as we waited for our teacher to arrive. They didn't have robes and seemed to be pretty typical mid-20 something New York City transplants. I took note, but didn't think much of it. I was all smiles and excitement as this would be my first direct experience with others on the path—or so I thought.

When the teacher walked in, just on time, she had a calm demeanor, smiling and nodding to everyone in the class. She was wearing a simple but long orange and yellow robe, and had some cloth wrapped around her head. She was likely in her early 40s, Caucasian, slender and a few inches shorter than I. She sat down and welcomed us.

After turning to the picture of her late teacher, offering him deep praise and gratitude, beckoning the class to do the same as she took us through a 20-minute meditation. It was the first time I had ever meditated in a group setting and I enjoyed being guided through a meditation that wasn't my own mind speaking to me or the voice of someone through headphones. That being said, it wasn't easy.

I struggled to stay focused with so many thoughts and questions bubbling in my mind. The people in this room were the only other Buddhists I had ever encountered, save from a few random street run-ins, and I had so much I wanted to talk about, share, and learn. When the meditation ended she launched into a story that related back to Buddhism, the Dali Lama, reincarnation, and how it applied to our own life. This was fine and all, but as she spoke, I began to notice something that didn't sit well with me.

From my understanding and personal experience of Buddhism, some things were so obviously clear that I had already, prior to going to that class, been "teaching" Buddhism to anyone that would listen. Just after a few months of teaching myself, I felt like I had a firm and clear grip on this 3000 year old teaching that had garnered hundreds of millions of followers over the years.

I felt comfortable enough sharing the benefits and the beauty of such a profound teaching and found that more often than not the only conversations I was interested in were around these topics. Premature I know, but there was something about discovering new pieces of life that affected me in such a profound way that I couldn't help but want to share it with anyone that might be open to it. It felt like I had been given a free gift, one that could profoundly help anyone, and I wanted to share that gift with as many people as possible.

One of the most important and essential of the Buddha's teachings was that what he attained could be attained by anyone willing to take a good hard look at the truth of the world, step beyond illusion, see where suffering came from, and pursue the path to free that suffering. To know this, he devised the four noble truths which are at the heart of his teaching.

This is a basic summary: First, there is suffering in life. Second, suffering has an origin. Third, suffering has an ending. And finally, there is a path to end that suffering. Another way to look at it in more basic terms is to imagine you had a sickness. You first discover you have a sickness because you have symptoms (your head hurts or you feel discomfort and pain). Then you have a diagnosis for that sickness; (headaches, depression, stress, the flu, etc). Then you have a treatment or a cure for that suffering (medication, meditation, therapy, etc.) depending on the sickness. And then, through following that treatment, you can cure your sickness. When it comes to "curing" your suffering from the Buddhist perspective, it is through a set of teachings that you can follow.

The suffering stuff may be at the heart of his teachings, but there is so much more. The Buddha spoke of unity with all, that all beings are interconnected, that there is, in truth, no separation between anything on the planet, that we are all one harmoniously connected mass of sorts existing together. Ironically enough it is science, through fields such as quantum physics, that has only recently started to uncover the truth of this statement. But, of course, so many people need the "scientific proof" to validate what the Buddha knew thousands of years ago.

One of the most valuable things I learned early on about his teachings, something I would come to find has become extremely controversial over the years and even hidden in most popular texts, is that no person has an individual soul. When I first read this, though a little bit confused that such a profound and spiritually inclined teaching would exclude the concept of a soul, I was open to what he said from a clear perspective. It made perfect sense to me.

What the Buddha taught was that the very idea that you can have an individual soul, a soul that is more than your flesh, that is uniquely yours, that essentially gains karma points as you go through life so that you can be reborn or elevated in the afterlife, was completely nonsensical and one of the main pieces to suffering.

The Buddha said this belief would separate you from the rest of the world, thus creating more pain and loneliness in your life. By thinking you have an individual soul, you would live a life of personal gain, doing all that you could to elevate your own needs to grow, grasping on to your individual identity instead of living in harmony with all of life.

He saw beyond that, knew that all of the world was connected, there were no individuals (only the attempt of the ego to keep us separate), that the world existed in one giant harmonious dance, and that we are all one. And that karma isn't a good or bad thing, but just the way that things are. Karma is essentially actions that are driven by intentions which lead to future outcomes.

You may often hear people talking about karma as though it's a tally point system; don't do that or you'll have bad karma, or do that, that's good karma. While in some ways there may be truth to that, it's often misrepresented. Karma is really just the natural order of the world, i.e. actions have reactions. They are not to be seen as a higher power judging people based on their actions, rather it is only the mind that places the label of 'good' or 'bad' upon them, which in itself is only a judgment that can often keep you stuck.

So, here I am sitting in this class, listening to the "teacher" speak when suddenly an uncomfortable feeling creeps into my heart as I notice the picture of the Dali Lama on a nearby wall. As it turned out, I was in a Tibetan Buddhism class, and in certain sects of Tibetan Buddhism they believe that the Dalai Lama, one with the original Buddha nature, is reincarnated continually on the planet time and time again into one new individual after the passing of the previous Dalai Lama.

While there are a lot of varying beliefs around this, the general idea is that the current Dalai Lama is a reincarnation of past Dalai Lamas. They are discovered through a series of tests, and in turn essentially become the new spiritual leader of the Tibetan Buddhist way. I'm not saying there is anything inherently wrong with the current Dalai Lama. He seemed like a peaceful, loving, sweet and super chill dude with a lot of good things to share, but it was the context that made me uneasy.

I did my best to stay until the remainder of class however, I suddenly felt little interest or desire to ask any questions or speak with anyone. When others in the class did begin to ask questions I started to notice how much the teacher was struggling to answer what I thought were very basic and simple teachings. I didn't want to say anything but rather observe the situation at hand. I knew something felt off, but I wasn't ready to speak up about it. It didn't make sense to me why the person teaching the class was considered the "teacher," seeing as how little of a grasp she seemed to have on the teachings.

What I slowly started to piece together was that she took on the role of the teacher simply because she had been studying Tibetan Buddhism longer than the 4-5 people there and thus was higher on the (probably plant-based) food chain.

When the class ended, I left and found a park bench to sit on in Union Square. I was feeling quite discouraged—the world around me suddenly felt gray and bleak once again. As I looked around at the bustling city of fast movers and shakers, all seemingly trying to get to the next thing-- grow their startup, climb the ranks of their corporation, or be discovered as the next big thing in the arts, I wondered how I could live out this peaceful and clear existence in such a crazy and chaotic place, especially when I felt that the Buddhists I just encountered even had missed the point.

That's when that old saying about New York City popped into my head. "If you can make it here, you can make it anywhere". Suddenly it was clear. I was meant to be here. If I could live out a peaceful, mindful and loving life in such an intense place, I could do it anywhere. This concrete jungle would be my training ground to break through the invisible barriers that were confining me.

A few weeks went by and after wondering if the first attempt was a fluke, I decided to go to another meditation class. This time I found one of a similar design right by my house, right in the heart of Hipster Land, Williamsburg. This class was packed full of about 25 people, a more diverse group of mostly new-age-type folk from around the world. After ten minutes or so of sitting patiently our teacher walked in. He was a tall, slender Caucasian man in his early 30's with a simple white flowing robe. I quickly wondered if this would be a little too similar to the juggling act I saw only weeks earlier in Union Square. Trying my best not to judge or make up stories, I sat back and allowed a pure state of presence to wash over me.

It started out the same, a blessing for his teacher followed by a guided meditation before opening up the room to questions. At first the questions were simple and the "teacher" gave some simple and thoughtful enough answers that kept most of the class smiling and comfortable enough to ask more of the bigger questions. He seemed to have a better grip on the teachings than the teacher of my previous class. But then a distraught woman with brown hair and a rigid face, in her late 30's, stood up and asked a question that swiftly smacked the smiles off of nearly everyone's face.

"How can Buddhism explain what happened to my friend?" She asked somewhat agitated. "You talk about peace and love and right action, but what can someone do when they are in a physically abusive relationship, when their partner beats them physically? How can your so-called enlightened Buddha explain and make sense of something so terrible as that?".

Radio silence...

The teacher was stumped. Clearly he could see how emotional this woman was getting and didn't know what to say. He stood there silently, straining to keep a smile, perhaps it was out of fear of making it worse, or perhaps it was one of those questions that he simply wasn't prepared to answer. However, I felt I was. Silly me.

A rush of clarity flowed through my body forcing me to stand up and I began to speak both to the "teacher" and the woman simultaneously, turning my head back and forth. I don't remember exactly what I said but I remember feeling confident as I spoke to her about how Buddhism involves some serious reflection and that while harmful and bad behavior should never be accepted or condoned and that no one ultimately deserves what your friend is going through, that the journey starts from within and that she had to start taking responsibility and thus action to get out of a bad situation and that blame and confusion were ultimately not going to help her get unstuck.

Midway through speaking, as I launched into my little rant, I looked around and was initially shocked to see glaring stares from nearly everyone in the class. I could only imagine what they were thinking but what I felt was something along the lines of, "How dare you speak, you are not our teacher, you don't have the faculty, you do not wear a robe, your face is not on the website. Who do you think you are speaking out of line?! This is not your place!".

It was in that moment that I realized what this class was all about. It wasn't about waking up to the truth, it was about following a very specific set of rules that existed in a hierarchy, basic things to make people feel just a little bit more comfortable, cozy and okay with their life. Fine and all, but ultimately more illusion. It seemed a heck of a lot more like a new type of religion, not the old type of religion many there had likely come to detest, but a more subtle and elusive one, not one aligned with the heart of Buddha's teachings. Silly me, truth aint for kids.

The more I looked, the more I saw that so much of present day Buddhism had turned into a religion of sorts. It wasn't about attaining

Buddhahood, which from my direct experience was available to anyone willing to pursue the great quest of truth, but more so about having something to follow that was more fluffy and gracious than what they were taught to believe growing up, bowing down to the master, being part of something seemingly great, but not being THE thing or seeing any clear way to get there.

I knew in my heart that the Buddha's teachings were available to any serious seeker and could ultimately lead to the end of suffering and the way of truth. Unfortunately what I saw here was something entirely different. I'm not saying it was wrong, I'm sure the people in the class and most that follow such teachings have mostly good intentions and are probably doing a lot of great things in the world, but I wasn't interested in becoming another sheep in the flock of followers, and I knew the Buddha hadn't been either. I knew it was completely counterintuitive to his teachings and would only keep people stuck in their slumbers. But as you may well know, a cozy sleep is an easy sell and I'd be damned to try and wake anyone up from that.

The final straw for me was after the class when the teacher invited anyone that had time for lunch at a Sushi place down the street. I couldn't exactly afford to eat sushi but I couldn't pass up a chance to talk to the teacher and a few students directly to see if I could get a better understanding of what was really going on. The lunch was fine, I don't remember much of the conversation, but the moment when one of the students said, "Isn't this so cool? Being Buddhist is the best religion, it is so much cooler than the others," I got up, thanked them for their time, and left never to go to another class like that again.

I was starting to feel more and more at a loss with Buddhism. The teachings to me were plain and simple, the Buddha just a man, like anyone else, that took some serious time and did some serious thinking to examine and make sense of the world beyond illusion, but his words had been clouded and distorted through the current human perspective. The interesting part to me was that the Buddha, living over 3000 years ago, could, like Jesus, be entirely myth. All that I had learned and appreciated about his teachings could be the work of a group of people hiding behind the veil of an enlightened being.

But that didn't matter to me because I knew very well that the teaching was in fact the thing that mattered and that the teacher didn't need to be real in order for me to know something to be true. Only I had to know it for myself. Anyone could attain what he spoke of, not through becoming an expert on the history or culture, wearing what he wore, eating what he ate, or smiling how he smiled, but by knowing it fully for themselves.

The Buddha, it seemed, was turned into a sort of bastardized version of himself in so many ways, a way to sell books, statues, incense, someone that people could put on a pedestal, or could put their faith in, even if that was completely misguided in his teachings. It seemed to keep people feeling safe, allowing for those that perhaps didn't believe in God to find solace in some other great being all while blinding themselves to the truth.

When I thought about it for too long I found myself frustrated by the whole thing, but in the end I also knew better and realized it wasn't my job or responsibility to convince someone otherwise. Who the heck was I to pretend like I had the answers for everyone? Just because I saw what seemed like a distraction, or a missed opportunity, didn't mean that my way was the only way. If something worked for someone, or they believed that they were on the path to something great, who was I to judge or care? It would only distract me from my own path ultimately. It was around this time that I discovered something in the most unlikely of ways that would shift my path forever and away from Buddhism.

Kill Kill Kill the Buddha—Until He is Dead

Over the course of my life, I have come to see the value and importance of diving into something fully. Not dipping my toe in the water, testing the temperature and then contemplating what it might be like when I dive in, but simply jumping in head first. Whether that be in a career choice, a relationship, or a teaching, I have found the best way to experience something fully is to dive right in, fear, trust, and all. But the thing about diving in head first is that in the moment when you are fully engulfed in its tantalizing flame it can feel like that thing is forever, like that relationship is all there ever is and will be, but I have seen that just because something seems perfect in a moment does not mean that it is meant to last forever.

And so rather quickly, after my somewhat off-putting experiences with Buddhism, I found myself dropping the teachings. I was reminded of something I learned early on in Buddhism where Gotama says, "Use my teachings as a raft to get you from one place to the next. Once you are on the other side of the river, do not hold the raft on your back as you continue on. Let it go." It was in this simple metaphor, one that is often overlooked, that I was reminded--once I learned and developed what was necessary to free myself from illusion and suffering, I had to move on.

I too admittedly had a little golden Buddha statue. I bought it early on as a sort of symbolic form of mindfulness. In my room I had a small wooden box where I would keep valuable things such as money and little notes from friends and past lovers and who am I kidding, my weed and a small bag of mushrooms. I placed the Buddha statue on top of the box so that each time I had to get something out of it I did a short little mindfulness practice where I slowly removed the statue, took what I needed, and placed it gently back in place. It was a way for me to think about the things I was taking out of the box, my intention for using them, and whether or not I really needed the thing in that moment.

One day, when I had just started to feel frustrated with some of what I recently experienced with present day Buddhism in NYC, I not-so-mindfully knocked the statue of the Buddha off my box, flinging it through the air. As it tumbled onto the ground the Buddha's head broke clean off. "Oh shit," I thought, and then as I remembered something I had recently discovered, I burst out laughing.

One of the most important parts of Buddhism was that

Gotama was just a man, not a god, no matter how much he may seem to be idolized as one. Along the journey to spiritual growth and enlightenment, to truly get anywhere, you must, at some point, cut off the head of your teacher, metaphorically of course (I, nor the Buddha I imagine, would ever suggest any physical act of violence). When we put people on a pedestal, when we look up to someone as though they are something greater than us, we automatically trap ourselves from any real growth, which is fine and all if we simply want to follow, but that is not what Buddhism is about, not at least how I had come to understand it.

It is more akin to attaining that which anyone who is a serious seeker can attain, not through intellect or intelligence, but through uncovering truth. And the same goes for me and this book, as I briefly mentioned earlier, I am just a person, I don't have anything special that you will never have. What I have uncovered about life is available to anyone willing to put in the time to look for themselves. Who are you idolizing in your world that may be keeping you stuck? Who are you bowing down to that may keep you from seeing the expansive greatness that you are? It could be a teacher, a guru, a master, a celebrity, a politician, the leading name in your field or even a friend or family member. (Perhaps now is another good time to do some writing of your own and dig into who that may be).

I kept my headless Buddha around as a swift reminder of the direction I was going, but I was starting to feel a strong pull away from anything spiritual, a pull to move forward with my life from this new place I had discovered and continue to invest my full efforts in music to see where that took me. For a few weeks it seemed to work out just fine, but then good old universe came a knockin' at my door.

As the sun sets in the distance,
it dances a sweet delight,
gently floating away to make room for night.
I watch with open eyes, mind still, heart aligned.
Suddenly all is clear,
the way to exist exists right here.

No longer do I sleep through the day,
rather I watch the sun come out to play,
and dance its fire dance so pure,
reminded me to move once more.

-*Yoshua*

During my first years in NYC I lived next to a group of 4 college students in an artists' loft in Williamsburg. We all quickly bonded and I felt it was a great opportunity for me to socialize and meet new people without having to go too far (about ten feet to be exact). Oftentimes when I would return home from work I would walk next door, maybe get handed a beer, or a blunt, and connect with whomever was over at the moment. We had a lot of fun together and although I wouldn't consider my neighbors to be spiritually inclined, I've come to learn that life can surprise you in the most unexpected ways.

One day after work I walked over to find one of their friends, Pat, sitting on a chair reading a book that caught my attention. There was something about the book that stood out in a way no other "spiritual" book had, I couldn't put my finger on it, but I felt a strong pull to find out what it was.

"What is that book you're reading?" I asked.

"Oh this, it's called Spiritual Enlightenment: The Damndest Thing," said Pat. "It's by this guy named Jed McKenna. He says he is enlightened but talks about how enlightenment isn't what we generally think of it as and that anyone can attain it. He lives in this big house, people come to visit and stay with him, and he talks to them about life and helps them wake up."

"That is interesting indeed," I replied in bewildered excitement as I took note of the title and immediately searched for a way to download and read it on my phone

Once the book started downloading via the app on my phone, I left almost immediately and began reading. I read and read and read, and I didn't stop, even on my way to the subway to take a meeting, I barely looked up from my phone as I read through the entire book almost without pause in less than a day. Suddenly everything had changed and my spiritual pursuit that had caused me to leave Buddhism was reawakened, but in a new way.

Here was this guy Jed, just a regular guy, who went out into the world, not totally unlike the Buddha, and uncovered what was true. He lived in Iowa in a communal house, a sort of accidental Ashram, where people lived and visited him to learn and talk about all sorts of spiritual, truth, and growth related matters but he didn't have any special teaching or a dogma he followed, he simply talked to people about how to hack away at the false world until you arrived at the ONLY truth.

Suddenly I felt a weird sensation, as if this book was the missing link to my own spiritual journey, the key to unlocking a piece that had been elusive up to that point . With each passing page Jed was confirming everything I had been feeling about new age spirituality, the misconceptions of "enlightenment" and "false gurus," and all. It was as if everything I had thought but couldn't properly express or put words to he had found a way to. It felt almost like Jed was writing directly to me as if to say, "Hey Josh, I know you feel alone in thinking what you know to be true, I am here to remind you that you are not alone, that what you see makes perfect sense, regardless of what others say or think about you".

Jed spoke of a process called Spiritual Autolysis, a name he coined for one of the key mechanisms and tools to shepherd the awakening process. It took me a few weeks to fully understand what he was referring to, but the more I thought about it I discovered I had essentially "accidentally" done it while in my car the months before, writing and deeply examining all of my thoughts, ideas and beliefs, until I got to something that was actually true. Jed also wasn't your average spiritual teacher. Yes, he referred to himself as "enlightened" but only because there isn't really a great way to explain what abiding non-dual awareness really is. He wasn't what you'd normally think of when picturing an enlightened person, but that is what made it make all the more sense to me. Jed was just a guy--a guy who shared his experience of uncovering the nature of reality, ate fish tacos, went skydiving, road bikes, played video games from time to time, wrote a book, and guided people who were often lost in a mess of spiritual bullshit.

Often times people that were still lost and struggling to find peace would come to him with all sorts of "wisdom" and experience from great masters and Gurus that they studied from for years on end. It was often a similar pattern--someone wanted to attain cosmic consciousness, they saw enlightenment as a state of total, all the time, bliss, like some never ending ecstasy high and wanted to know why their practicing had led them astray. Jed would listen to their story and attempt to redirect them. He would see that they were going in the wrong direction, that they were being distracted by the fluffy and shiny stuff, and show them that real enlightenment wasn't a pretty process, but more attuned to spiritual warfare, waging a war on the false-self that keeps us feeling stuck and separate, burning it all to the ground until only truth is left.

From my lens everything he said made perfect sense,

not because I blindly believed it, but because I knew it deep within my heart. He confirmed all that I had felt but didn't know how to express, and previously had had no one to turn to or to talk to about. I wasn't so much learning new things as I was aligning with what I had already known. It all clicked when I was able to see it on paper. Enlightenment isn't about learning more so much as it is about unlearning what is not true, stripping away falsehood to get to the heart of what really is. It may sound strange but a part of me felt like future me had written the book and sent it to present me to validate all that I had known but couldn't fully articulate.

One thing I appreciated about his approach was that he shared relatable metaphors and even used popular stories like the Matrix to demonstrate the awakening process. Neo is living in a world where something just doesn't feel quite right, he knows there is more but has no one to confirm or deny his beliefs, so he goes about doing what he does until one day he gets the call.

Morpheus reaches out to him and tells him about the Matrix. Neo doesn't exactly know what it is but he knows it is something big. Deep within his body he has always felt that things were not quite as they seemed. After getting all the confirmation he needed, he is taken on a journey, red pill or blue pill, to be shown the truth of the world. He is shown that he has been living in a computer simulation of sorts, in a false world, and that the real world exists for those willing to see it. The real world isn't necessarily better, or prettier or happier, but it is real, and Neo knows he can't unsee what he has seen and that he must follow this new path down the Rabbit hole.

Yes, the movie has action packed scenes, guns a-blazing, and all of the drama you'd hope for in a Hollywood blockbuster, but the deeper story rings true in many ways to the awakening process and if you go back and rewatch it, as I have many times from this perspective, you may just see it in a whole new way. It is only one way to explain the awakening process and there are many others, but regardless they all lead back to the same truth that I had discovered months before in my car; all beliefs are just that, beliefs. None are true. Opinions on top of opinions, ideas and perspectives held up by no more than an illusion of right and wrong, a world built on beliefs about what people should and should not do, not from a place of knowing, but from a place of fear and guess work. Trying to share these concepts without muddying them with more beliefs of my own can make it quite challenging to write about if you know what I mean. But alas, all we have are words to communicate that which cannot really be communicated through words, so here I am giving it a shot. And if you know what I mean, if you can see that the great paradox of life is hidden within the words we use to define it, then you might just take a moment to smile.

I Don't Exist

Two things happened after I read the book that blew my mind to bits. First off, after my first read, I could not get enough of what I was ingesting and decided to re-read the entire book again. The book was digital on my phone so I scrolled back to start from page one and to my amazement all of the pages were blank. *What the fuck?* I scrolled through page after page, nothing... I deleted the book, re-purchased it even downloaded it all over, and yet again all of the pages were blank. Now, this was the early days of the iPhone. I had the first generation, so it would be easy to blame it on technology, but I couldn't help but see the deeper meaning of it all as I thought about one of my favorite Buddhist teachings; *Use my teachings as a raft you blind fool!* (okay maybe I altered it slightly)

It was the only sign I needed to move forward with my life and not grasp on too deeply to what Jed had shared, and thus the words were blank. I needed to take what I had learned, apply it, and move on. That being said, as the weeks went by, I was curious to learn more about Jed so I started doing some digging on the internet. To my amazement I discovered that he had written two other books in a trilogy series and eventually I ordered the second book many months later when I felt ready to pick it back up. But that wasn't what surprised me, it was what I learned about Jed Mckenna that shattered my world.

As it turned out, Jed McKenna—the author of what had quickly become the most life altering book in my life—did not exist. *Wait what?* Yes, Jed was made up, a ghost writer, and no one knew a single thing about him. He was not an actual spiritual teacher, just a pen name, had no book tours, and no workshops or lectures to sign up for. Not even the ashram style house where he met students in his book seemed to be real—though I can't say for sure. At first I was disappointed and extremely confused. I wanted to meet him, talk to him, learn more from him, get a better sense of his life story, but alas, he was not real and there was nothing I could do about it.

After pondering this for a short while it all began to make perfect sense. Jed was not trying to write a book as a spiritual teacher searching for praise, accolades, or recognition, rather his words were only meant to be a reflection into truth, a way for the reader to see themselves and not get distracted by the person behind the words. *Like a finger pointing at the moon*, as Jed McKenna often talked about, do not get caught up in the finger that is doing the pointing or you'll never get to the moon.

What made the fact that Jed was made up so fascinating to me was only becoming more clear the more I thought about what he shared about his perspective on new age spirituality and its foundation of materialism as a way to sell things and often feed the ego of the teacher. This is not to say that Jed himself wasn't selling books, but they were used as a tool to help wake people up, not to feed his ego or grow some sort of following. He doesn't do press around the books, or have social media, or anything like that, he doesn't exist, and so all that you read in the book is reflected back on you.

Anything that you feel, think, or come to understand is of your own experience and not to be tangled up with the teachings of another, filtering through your own experience of life. It's been ten years since I first read the book and though I've given it to hundreds of people, until very recently I had never met anyone that had even heard of Jed Mckenna, I suppose you could say the teacher shows up when you are ready.

The Outsider

Early on, during all of this spiritual awakening (or whatever the hell you want to call it, heck you could call it "flippity-floppity," considering no word can really capture what it is anyhow) stuff, though I felt disconnected from so many people in my life, I was fortunate enough to have one of my best friends, John Clay to talk to about it all.

John, or Clay as we call him, a 5'10, light brown haired, blue eyed, medium built, tattoo covered, Christian raised boy, with a heart warming smile, and I have become best friends but were not close in High School. Even though we attended a fair amount of classes together and were both on the football team, we only ever really spoke in passing. Ryan and our other pal Bogan used to rave about how funny and enjoyable I was to hang out with but Clay and our other pal Bub were always confused because the Josh they knew was quiet and shy.

"Uh, Josh? Really? Him?" said Clay. "I mean he seems like a nice guy but..."

What Clay and Bub hadn't realized was they only knew the Josh in school and on medication, the not fun, quiet, comedically repressed, robotic Josh that was rather boring at best. It would be a few years later in college when I traded my medication for music, started a band and got my humor back that we would get much closer. Although we started to develop a deep bond years before through music and making each other laugh our assess off, it took us a few years to connect on another level as we realized that we were both into all of this higher consciousness and truth. stuff.

Reading the Jed books, as well as perusing through countless books and other mind-altering written sources, together was an opportunity for us to share insights, openings and paradigm shifts that we were going through. The trick, we found, was finding a balance between being serious and even scholarly about it at times, and yet catching ourselves and each other when we started to take it too seriously (or even get a little high and mighty about it), only to reel it all in with the humor of it all.

Bringing in the lightness and cracking silly jokes whenever the moment was right was a way to cut the often times heaviness that gets roped in to a lot of what is considered spiritual. After all, as "serious" as this stuff might seem, it's also one big hilarious fuggin joke, and I mean that in the best way possible. Life is hilarious. The very nature of reality, the attempt we make at being a "real" character in the world, even when you actively know it is all made up—flat out hilarious.

As I experienced my own awakening (man, sometimes that word gets to me, but why care really, it's just another word) I can't deny there were times where I felt a little crazy and I'll be damned if it didn't help to have a friend, even just one or a few, that understood. Even if YOU, as you read on, start to feel isolated and alone in the world, remember that I am but a friend here to remind you that it's all good. And no, I don't mean it like an invisible friend, although, to each their own!

Through countless conversations that I've had with people of all walks of life, I have come to find that most humans in the world, at one point or another, feel disconnected, alone, like an outsider, or as though they simply don't fit in anywhere (and funny that I should be reading this very sentence after having just re-watched Joker). Subsequently they often shut down, step back into their character, play their assumed role, and try and forget about what they saw.

But I, as someone who could not unsee the truth no matter how hard I tried at first, have felt a deep calling to share this with others. Not for praise or acknowledgement, I have learned enough about that world to know it has no real intrinsic value or benefit to me (even though that was part of an earlier desire of mine), but simply because I know how powerful it was to have direction and support in that seemingly dark, confusing and scary place. I suppose in a way it's not unlike the whole "pay it forward" thing—aaaaand I'm fine with that.

If what you are reading ring true, if you feel alone, like you don't fit in, like you've seen something that no one else seems to get, let these words be a reminder that you are not alone. You may feel like the exception, the outcast, crazy, out of your fuggin mind even (and perhaps in the confines of societal norms you are), but that isn't a bad thing. To feel "out of your mind," however negative sounding that may be, is probably more attuned to the awakening process than the standard alternative of trying to "stay in your mind," when you really think about it.

I should mention that it's one thing to feel alone in what you are discovering, but it is another to question your own sanity. I would say that you shouldn't but that is a flat out lie—you most certainly might and likely will. It's easy to feel crazy during the process of awakening to the reality of the world—trying to fit into a system, a box, that doesn't make sense and is based on lots of lies and fear.

It is in the trying to fit in to a broken system that gives us the illusion that there is something wrong with us, especially when everyone else around us seems perfectly fine (ha!). But that is simply not the case, rather simply something to be aware of. I, having experienced it first hand, most certainly know. I sometimes imagine a sliding door moment in my life, a parallel reality, where I completely lost my marbles and never made sense of what was happening to me.

It's almost funny how easily being awake could be misinterpreted for being bat shit crazy under the wrong circumstances. Which brings me to a story about another friend that woke up in the most unlikely of ways.

The Truman Show Wall

Regardless of what I heard about with Jed and the various types of people that come to him as seekers, I still believed to some degree that waking up was solely a spiritual pursuit and that by being on the "spiritual path," by reading books, going to the events, and you know, doing all "the things," that one could find what they were truly looking for if all the cards lined up.

Because of that I still had some past conditioned beliefs that told me in order to see the truth, to become aware and awake, that some level of mindfulness, meditation, or reading and writing of the spiritual nature was necessary to get there and would likely be the spark that ignited the path. It seemed somewhat logical, for how could one find growth on the spiritual path without being on it? Yes, It made perfect sense, that was until I reconnected with a friend recently and opened my mind yet again to a judgment I hadn't realized was still there.

I've known Sophia for the last 15 year. We grew up in the same town, had a similar enough upbringing, and though we never spoke all that much or connected on a personal level, we had a strong connection through music that kept us in touch. Not all that long ago I got a message from Sophia and felt called to ask how life was treating her.

"I don't know where to begin," she said. "I hit the Truman show wall, I may sound mental but you may feel me on this, I have an instinct you may."

To which I replied, "You don't sound mental, you sound sane, to not see the thin veil of truth hiding amongst the boxes of fear is the mental thing."

I shared a bit about what was going on with me, how I had been in this space for quite some time, and how I had literally just had a conversation that day with someone about the Truman show and the false world and what not. A day or so later she replied saying, "I am in tears, I'm gonna take this as a universe sign and that's cause it feels that way, we should talk."

We ended up getting on a call a few days later and she filled me in on everything that had happened in the past few months of her life. Before our conversation, admittedly there were things that I expected to hear her say, parts of her story that I imagined to be similar to so many others I met going through a similar transition, but boy was I wrong.

Sophia went on to share that earlier in the year her partner cheated on her and that it sent her into a downward spiral of darkness and depression. She felt stuck in the relationship even though rationally she knew it should be over but didn't know what to do to break her emotional connection to him. She started to read about quantum physics, searching for something to make sense of her situation, and then, seemingly out of nowhere, something happened that changed her life forever.

On March 4th, in a dark place, she went out to party with friends and drank way too much, pushing herself into a state of complete inebriation and ultimately blacked out. The next day when she woke up, instead of feeling terribly hungover as she expected she would be, she felt light and clear. Everything had changed, the heaviness she had felt in the days before was gone, she saw everything from a different perspective, the emotional attachment to her partner was gone, she even stopped smoking cigarettes when only the day before she was completely addicted.

She could suddenly see through everything, the false-world, the characters, the veil. It was all shattered. She wasn't on a spiritual path, she had no interest in anything spiritual, and yet overnight her entire life changed in a way she could never have imagined.

Sophie, without fully understanding what was happening to her, didn't experience people the same way she did only the day before. She didn't have the same attachments she once had, the same frustrations, the same confusions. It's not to say that everything went away in an instant, even though the feeling and the awareness was radical and has only heightened since, but rather that something was revealed to her, something she had not seen before, something she wasn't even looking for or interested in, became clear, a false weight was lifted.

It may have just been the beginning of her journey, one that she didn't plan to go on, but she knew her life was different and that she could never go back. It would be the moment that set her on a new path, one where she started to see things for what they were, not what they were supposed to be.

We talked for a good few hours and I assured her that while she may feel isolated at times in the processes of coming into alignment with truth, over time her world would continue to make more and more sense and she would continue to meet other folks she could relate to.

One thing I found both fascinating and interesting as I have been talking to Sophia fairly often since we reconnected, was that she understood quite simply the non-duality of life and consciousness in a way that so many others that I've met searching hard for clarity, doing all of the "right" and "spiritual things," did not. I am not sharing this story to suggest you go get black out drunk in the hopes of achieving some level of "awakening" (wouldn't that be something), but rather that there is no one way to go about the process and who knows, perhaps you are already in it without knowing it, not unlike Sophia.

It is interesting for me, as I think of her experience, to reflect back on my own journey. While I did take somewhat of a "spiritual path" in one regard, my clarity and awakening really came when I was at my lowest and darkest, not when I was trying to only call in "high vibes" or whatever the heck. Truth can come knocking at your door at any time and may even surprise you how it shows its face. That being said, just because you might start to see things differently, doesn't mean the work is done and life is suddenly in flow, but it's that first step that can set you up for what is to come and point you in the right direction.

"That can't be possible? *What do you mean we're in California? We were headed to New York City by way of Colorado. We had a great plan, detailed directions, and we put in so much effort driving and staying focused.*"

"*I know dear, we did so good and tried so hard, but also, we drove the wrong way the whole time!*"

"*The whole time? THE WHOLE TIME!?*"

The awakening process has nothing to do with any one specific, rule laden, path, no matter how right one road might seem on the surface (i.e. moving to a monastery, shaving your head, and eating only rice for 5 years). Not even reading books, meditating and decorating your house more spiritually means much of anything from a misguided view and with the wrong intention. Those things can be helpful in some ways and may work for you, but they hold no definitive value and in many ways can be a hindrance and a cage—just as blaming everything going wrong in your life on the moon cycle can be. No matter how hard you try, if you are going the wrong direction you will never get to where you think you're headed.

Sometimes the people that seem and act the most "spiritual" are the most full of crapola, hiding behind the illusion that wearing flowing clothing and saying namaste all the time is actually going to mean anything even if they haven't done the work. It sounds nice, and it may even be nice, but is often a way for people to cover up what is really hiding deep inside—a scared shitless child trying to make sense of a cruel world. And yet it is that child inside of all of us that we can meet anew and help to grow the heck up.

Whatever personal choices, be it clothing, food or other, that you make, are of your own accord. I don't hold any judgment for what someone chooses to do with their time on this planet, and damned if there aren't an endless sea of possible things to do. The only reason I share is because all of these surface and material elements to spirituality can be a distraction from getting to the real stuff, and can be the thing that makes you feel like you are not worthy or part of the "in" crowd simply because you aren't attuned to dress or eat a certain way.

It's like the first time I went to a yoga class. Damn if I wasn't insecure about my body in ways I could never have imagined—do you really have to have a perfect body BEFORE ever doing yoga to do yoga? Dang.

If you take a good hard look at yourself, see beyond the veil of illusion, recognize the character you were raised to play in this world, and then, piece by piece, dissect and unravel that character that has been keeping you stuck, then you are clear to do as you please from a place of truth, not from what others tricked you into believing from their own fears and judgments. Once you've unpacked all of that, by all means wear, share, do, and talk about whatever feels right to YOU. But be careful not to get too caught up in the surface stuff, assuming that the pursuit of truth and spirituality has a dress code or only hangs out in certain places.

Once you've taken the first step, recognized in yourself that there is something greater than what you were told to believe, and that the cost of truth is everything, the digging only begins the process. Releasing and dissolving everything you know to be true, as I did, may be a way to help you tug on that thread and unravel untruth, or maybe it happens another way, but after, as I have personally come to experience through my own accord and the guidance of many teachers, there is still a long period of adjustment.

Manifesting desires, being in flow and at one with the universe, and all of the "perks" (or are they pleasant side effects?) that may come with waking up don't necessarily just magically become easier. There is still a long process of adjusting to the new world you are inhabiting, and it can still get painful, lonely and scary at times which may seem confusing. It is also quite lovely and blissful and joyous too, but from my experience there is no fully always blissed out state attuned to the likes of tripping balls all day long. Those altered states of consciousness are great, and I enjoy going into them from time to time, but being awake is something far simpler than that and is neither good nor bad, it simply is.

The only real difference between me and someone not in this way of being is that I'm fully aware that I am the thing that I am and always have been (you know, my divine nature and what not), and someone else might not yet be aware that they too are already that thing that they've always been. In truth, you can't not be what you always have been and always are, but the great illusion of fear, ego and falsehood can be pretty damn convincing.

Reading about the awakening process can be extremely challenging and triggering, especially if you yourself have spent countless hours on a spiritual path without getting as far as you'd expected. Maybe you've studied with a guru who you have a deep admiration and respect for and don't plan on giving up your connection to that person's teachings, and if so, that is perfectly fine. If what you are learning has been helpful and you really recognize the value in what you're experiencing and creating in your life, I wouldn't pretend to ask you to change anything, only to remind you to filter them from your own perspective, to see where perhaps you've missed something that could be a key to moving forward.

However, if you look around at that teacher and start to feel like something is off, start to wonder why the teacher seems to be in one place and none of the students have ever seemed to get there. If you recognize that they are only beyond you in their years of training, intellect and spiritual hierarchy, well then, you might have some more digging to do. There is nothing inherently wrong with studying "under" someone or learning from them, just be careful to not put that person on a pedestal and think they are something that you are not, for that is the great illusion. You can have deep respect and admiration for a human being, even be inspired by them, just as I have been by so many humans, but recognize that they are only a beacon to show you what is possible.

When you wake up, however gradual or quick it may happen for you, as it already may have, you will likely start to look around at the world and feel more and more isolated, as if everyone around you is watching a movie on repeat, continuing to feed a character that you now have come to see is not real. It can be extremely lonely and weird (as I have shared before and will keep drilling in the point), and your first inclination might be to try and shake people awake as I did. *Don't you see? This is a dream, this is not real, you are only pretending, you are an actor on a stage that believes the movie you are in is reality when it fact it is not!*

And while this may work as well as trying to catch a salmon swimming upstream with your bare hands while standing naked in Alaska in the dead of winter, I have found it's much easier to focus on your process and know that over time you'll find people in this space that you can relate to and have conversations that will not feel forced, but instead flow freely and excite you to your core. Maybe this book is the first of those conversations, or maybe you've had many, whatever it may be, you are not alone, just keep on moving, trust yourself and know that the more you align with your true nature, the more you will channel your inner divine guidance and flow with the universe's perfect design.

As Jed McKenna expresses quite simply in his book, you can awaken within the dream or you can awaken from it. And the thing about awakening from the dream is that it's not a conscious decision, it's not something you choose to do because it seems exciting, it's something that you can't avoid once it gets started, something you can't fully grasp until you've done it.

Once you start to unwind your dream state character and the dream you have been living in, the process practically takes care of itself. You might, along your journey, stop off at some lovely destinations, check out the sites, take a few pictures, as I did on many occasions, but if you are meant to keep going, something deep down will continue to push, excuse me, hurl you forward no matter what the cost.

I don't bring this up to convince you to do anything different from what you are already doing, only to express that if you feel like the new and sweeter life you are attempting to live in starts to feel equally uncomfortable at some point, even if it felt great for years, that that is a natural part of the process. Once you've woken up to truth, you start to shift from one state of not knowing, to a state of perfect knowing. It might only take an instant to achieve "enlightenment" (or whatever the hell you want to call it), but it could take years, if not a lifetime to adjust to, and in many cases even realize that that is what it is.

That doesn't mean your life is instantly great and that you feel some endless high all of the time, but that when it becomes clear you exist in truth and align with the flow of the universe. Once you are there, you can drop the teachings, even the practices if you want, or keep them, it no longer matters, you no longer need to hold on to things. Attachment and non-attachment are non-issues, there is no real question about whether you are doing things right or wrong, because you exist from a deeper knowing.

Once the false-self has been dissolved, the ego ended, what once seemed scary, bleak, hopeless, is suddenly exactly as it should be. It's not easy to describe what the state is like, it certainly doesn't take for a good sales pitch; "That's right ladies and gentleman, for the price of everything you love you could have nothing at all, all you have to do is annihilate everything you think you know and believe". Which is why people don't choose this, and why it can feel far easier to avoid it at all costs and do whatever it takes to stay asleep, swapping a bad dream for a better one perhaps. And you most certainly can and should if that feels right to you, I couldn't, however I tried, and fuck if it didn't seem like a nice alternative at times.

But on the other side of everything, when you align with all that is, a new space opens up, one where you know, beyond anxiety, doubt and fear, what you are meant to do at any given time. You don't judge or over think what needs to be done because you know that whatever you do is the thing to do. Even if you slip up for a moment, as I have many times, or have a brief encounter with fear, the second you stop to think about it, you see it for what it is and the feeling goes away.

Some of your most cherished and beloved spiritual practices may even go as they stop serving you, just as the Buddha expressed dropping the teachings like dropping the raft. Sure, losing it all seems unthinkable before you have, but once you have, after you start to adjust, you realize that what you've always wanted was nothing at all.

When I look at spirituality from the physical and material world, it seems that it is a path for the few, but ultimately, on a much simpler and energetic level, the pursuit of truth and the awakening process is one that we are all on together always. During this thing we call life we do our best to make sense of the world around us, learning from others, rebelling against what we've learned, sticking to what works, or finding something new when it doesn't. Our misguided mind is often the thing that gets in the way, the thing that convinces us we are either doing a good or bad job, all while keeping us stuck in a monotonous loop with no clear ending.

Take a moment to pause and realize that you are exactly where you need to be, that the thinking brain, however good a tool it may be, is just a tiny piece of the infinite everythingness and nothingness that you are.

You are, in this moment, and every moment before and after, everything that ever has and will be, you need only look beyond the ego to be reminded of this. Being in vibrational harmony with the totality of your being might sound like a big and long pursuit, but time and space are relative and you are already there, always. Keep searching to dismantle the false within, to trim away the fat and fear that is not you, and you'll see just how clear life becomes when you remember that you are not fighting against the world around you, but that you are in direct connection and oneness with everything that is and always will be.

It may feel different than you imagined it to but simply by taking a moment to pause, to temporarily stop the doing and sit with yourself for a moment, taking in the universe around you, you just might start to notice that all is consciousness, and that you are always at one with it all. No matter how hard you do or do not try to be there, all that you see, all that you experience, taste, touch, and feel, is as much a part of you as everything.

From my experience Jed and the Buddha were two figures (whether real or not) that really helped me to make sense of what I was going through on my journey, but there have been plenty of other people, places and things that have taught me exactly what I needed to hear in the exact right moment. They say that the teacher shows up when the student is ready and while I appreciate that sentiment, it took me a long time to realize that the teacher can show up in all forms—a human, a book, an animal, a blade of grass—when we see life as it is, every single morsel of existence can teach us the secrets of the universe.

(Just a side note, if you feel like you've had an awakening in your mind, and that all of this makes sense, but feel that your physical body has not caught up and find that you keep falling into the same fear based patterns, I share more about trauma and the emotional side of awakening in the chapter, "On Lying, Telling the Truth and Honesty.")

Five

On Death, Consciousness and Other Things We Share in Common

Death:

The action or fact of dying or being killed; the end of the life of a person or organism

Consciousness:

The state of being awake and aware of one's surroundings

Aware:

Having knowledge or perception of a situation or fact.

To this day, I'm still on the fence about whether or not I died at the age of 11, and yes—I know how that sounds. I want to take a moment to share a story with you that very well may have been the thing that changed my life's path forever.

With winter break nearly upon us, it was the first snowy day of the season. I was dressed in khaki pants, a white button up shirt and a blue blazer. It was the day of the big school play. I had a small part in a Christmas Carol, I was the butcher and had only one or two lines, but I was excited as this was a big deal for me. David, a boy of my age, brown hair, slim build, about my size, who was my best friend at the time, and I walked side by side to the bus stop as we did each school morning. But this morning was different, it was snowing and our walk was more slippery than usual.

When we got to the bus stop David walked over to the large crab apple tree to search for some fruit to toss and knock some more crab apples down, a fun game we used to play. For whatever reason instead of joining in with him as I usually did I decided to simply stand by the light post and wait for the bus. I remember the roads were a bit icy as the large snowflakes melted down onto my rosy red cheeks.

Suddenly, out of nowhere I looked up to my left and saw a red pick-up truck approaching from the near distance. Having lost control on the icy roads it was swerving back and forth. I remember standing there frozen, watching as it headed directly towards me. One moment I was watching, when suddenly everything went black.

The next thing I remember was opening my eyes as my body spun around on the ground, gradually coming to a halt. As my vision slowly came into focus everything was extremely bright—the snow, the light, I felt like I was coming back, but not necessarily to where I had just been moments before. I remember a medium built, middle aged African American man, wearing a warm blue jacket getting out of his car, which crashed into me and sent me flying to the ground before plowing into the street light and smashing it apart, trembling and saying, "Are you okay?"

"Yes," was all I replied as I slowly started walking home.

"Holy shit! Holy shit! What is going on?" Said David. "You just got hit by a car! I saw the whole thing! Are you okay?".

"Yes, I'm fine," I said in a soft and gentle tone. "I need to go home".

David ran back and grabbed my book bag and followed me home, he was in shock, I suppose I was too, but I also felt completely clear. When we got home and told my mom naturally she flipped out, wanting to know what the heck had happened, how I was, who had hit me and where he was. Somehow, and I can still hardly believe this, even with David screaming that I got hit by a car and how crazy it was, I managed to persuade my mom to let me go to school that day so that I could do my part in the play.

Soon after, when we did go to our family doctor and they examined me I seemed to be mostly fine, in a bit of a shock and bruises on my left arm, but I was released shortly after and told simply to rest. Maybe it was because I was barely injured, or perhaps because it was so odd, but little was spoken of my being hit by a car experience since then and as I tucked it away in my memory, it began to fade into a dream. Regardless, it was a huge moment in my life and took me over 20 years to start to understand, process and piece together what may have happened, all of which I will share, but first, a bit on death.

Scared to the Bone

The first time I ever thought about what dying really meant I must have been no more than seven or eight years old and it shook me to my core. My parents planned a vacation to Disney World and I was excited, but it was my first time ever getting on a plane. The day before we were slated to leave I froze in terror thinking about the unimaginable; DEATH!

For reasons that I will never remember, I was lying on the couch thinking about what being on an airplane might be like when suddenly I started thinking about what would happen if the plane crashed, which, in turn, led me to freaking out as I began to think of my own death. Not being someone who was raised in a very religious household, and being more scientifically inclined as a child, death to me meant the end of everything, that I would cease to exist, for all of eternity, that there would never be me again, my body lying stiff in a coffin underground for ever and ever and ever.

Needless to say it freaked my child mind out and cut a deep and painful scar in my subconscious as I shook back and forth, crying my eyes out, fearing for not only my own life, but the ending of all existence. I feared the blank, bleak, empty nothingness that I was certain would one day be my reality for infinity. As a boy growing up in a world where I was told to be tough, where boys don't cry or share their feelings, I feared what might happen if I told anyone, and so I kept it to myself, burying these fears deep down, and of course—only making it worse.

Before things take a darker turn, I'm not here to tell you that my perspective has stayed the same as that seven year old boy all of those years ago pondering the end of existence. Luckily, if luck is really a thing (which it most luckily isn't), I have managed to discover a much more clear and digestible view of what death really is, not from belief, religion or assumption but from dissecting what is and uncover what is most certainly not.

For me to fully explain what I now know death to be I have to back up a little bit and share a few things as we piece this elusive puzzle together. If you've ever heard the phrase "your mind creates your reality," and if you've done enough research or read enough books about it, you may have a grasp as to where this is going, or at least a few fundamental tools to get you there. If not, no worries, I will do my best to explain something that may seem complex but once it clicks it is actually quite simple and straightforward.

While it seems obvious, from a classically scientific perspective, that our brain controls our body and that our senses take in all the information around us, creating patterns and images in our minds that we then process into thoughts and what have you, the deeper you dive into quantum physics, relativity, and even Buddhism, the more you discover that there are other perspectives of reality that shine a light on so much of what we, as a human race, have struggled to understand for thousands of years—the great mystery of death and what happens to "us" when we die.

Just a mini refresher; If we go back around 3000 years to the time when the Buddha was said to have walked the earth, he uncovered that we were not separate individuals but that we were all connected beings, sharing in this earth, that there was no individual, but one ever changing, flowing organism, and by seeing the world as it was, and not as we were told to believe it was, that we could free ourselves from suffering. By taking on this perspective we could see that we were all connected to something greater than any one individual.

Thoughts arise in the mind, we experience things internally and those things are reflected externally to our outside world. In this way the external could be seen as an illusion, not so solid, but a mere reflection of our internal state of being, almost like a movie or painting to experience our physical life through.

Flash forward thousands of years to Albert Einstein. While he is known for a wide range of scientific breakthroughs and discoveries (as well as failures and missteps), the one that I find the most fascinating, and the most simple, is the concept of relativity. Einstein theorized that all things were relative to the observer, that there was no one specific truth, but that truth was relative to the person experiencing it.

The simplest way he put it was to imagine that you were on a train, and the train was moving rather fast. As you stand on the train you drop a ball, bouncing it up and down, catching it each time and dropping it once more. What you see is that the ball goes straight down, hits the floor and bounces right back up in your hands. The ball moves up and down in a uniform fashion. However if someone was standing on the ground, not on the train, as the train was passing, and if the train had floor to ceiling glass windows, what they would see as you dropped the ball to the ground was not that the ball went right up and down, but that it went down and up in a curving pattern, as they are seeing the train and the ball move from left to right as the ball is dropped up and down.

The point Einstein was making was that all things are relative to the observer, that there is no one inherent truth, but that the person seeing the experience can have a very different experience than someone else seeing it from a different perspective. On a simpler level, one person might think a movie is funny, another may not, it's all relative to the person and how they experience the movie, a matter of opinion, preference, their internal belief system and conditioned responses, their mood that day or perhaps whether or not they just ate a double cheeseburger before the film. Even the most praised critics that get paid the big bucks to review movies, regardless of what they say, is still their relative opinion. Einstein was on to something and while he explained it in mostly scientific terms, you can see it wherever you look.

Which brings us to Quantum Physics, a rather complex and

impressive sounding word if one was perhaps only hearing about it for the first time, but rather a simple concept in its most basic form. Without getting into too much of the specifics (with a quick search you can check out "double slit experiment" and "quantum entanglement" videos), the basic theory is that all matter, energy and particles that make up everything physical in this world, first exist as waves of potential.

To bring this down to an even simpler level (I know how "wave of potential" might sound), Imagine that the book, or electric device, you are holding right now as you read this, isn't actually solid. To all of your senses, it is quite real, right? It feels solid, you can see, touch it, even smack it against your head, and heck, it might even hurt a bit (do at your own risk). To all of your senses, it is extremely solid, and to think otherwise may seem crazy. Luckily I like a little crazy, they always bring something special to the party, don't they? But according to quantum physics, it's not so farfetched. While we see and feel and experience life as solid, all life exists as a wave of potential, and it is our mind and our senses that create a solid form of reality. Part of what the double slit experiment discussed in greater detail than I will, is that matter exists in physical form only when it is being observed.

In other words, all that we see, smell, taste, touch and see, while it is extremely convincing and seemingly obviously real, is only apparent in our mind and perceivable experience. As we interact with it, it appears, feels, and seems very solid and real. When we are not interacting with it, when we are not observing it, touching it, seeing it, being in direct contact with it, it only exists as potential, as though it could exist anywhere at any time, in any moment.

This may sound a bit trippy, or out there, but what is interesting is that these concepts that were originally more based on mysticism and spirituality, are starting to become heavily studied and deeply respected on a scientific level. Now, I'm not one to preach science over anything else, anything designed by humans is inherently susceptible to falling apart under direct scrutiny. And for as much as science seems to have the "answers" to so much, everything in science is openly considered a leading theory until another theory comes along and disproves the original. Science may have strong evidence one way or another around a belief, but there is never any 100% proof, because there is always doubt, no matter how real something seems.

But it just goes to show that everything converges at some level and no matter what field you approach something, it all comes from the same place. If you want to learn more about quantum physics there are a plethora of books, my favorite being "The Holographic Universe," by Michael Talbot, but feel free to go down the rabbit hole as you see fit.

And speaking of the Holographic Universe, I might as well

explain it in its most basic context. Have you ever seen a hologram? The basic idea is that if you take holographic film and take a picture of a solid object with it, such as a candle, then take that film and shine a light through it, what you'll see is a hologram of the candle that appears to be almost three dimensional. But what is fascinating about holographic film is that if you cut off a small piece of the film, say you cut the picture into 10 smaller squares, if you were to shine a light through any one of those much smaller squares, you'd actually still get a hologram of the entire image, not 1/10th of it. The image starts to fade the more you cut, but you still get the full image.

The holographic universe theory is that our world exists much more like a hologram than anything else, each part of existence contains the whole of everything. In other words, like the Buddha spoke of thousands of years ago, everything is connected, you exist as the totality of everything, not a separate individual as you believe yourself to be. And if everything is connected, our universe, our consciousness, everything that we experience, is all part of one greater whole. We are not separate individuals, but one interconnected experience. And the Buddha didn't need proof, he experienced a much deeper knowing, and only asked, as I do, for you to try it on for yourself.

To circle back into quantum physics and relativity—your mind is taking in the world around you, filtering it through all of your senses, thoughts, ideas, beliefs, and experiences, and painting a very real looking picture of life based on its ability to do so. But that picture may be, and most likely is, tainted in many ways. Your fears, judgments, beliefs and past experiences are all shaping what you experience in the now, and what you attract in the soon to be. You may be familiar with the law of attraction, but we attract far more than we ever realize because we are constantly and always creating reality as we experience it. It's easy to ignore this, the very idea that you are in control of your life can be scary, like too much responsibility, but knowing this can also be empowering because anything is possible when you understand that you are limitless energy and potential.

One interesting thing in the science world is that scientists (though of course not all, I am generalizing) are trying, in every which way, to create a Theory of Everything, or TOE for short. The TOE attempts to figure out a unified formula that can explain everything in the known universe, and so far it has had little luck in doing so. Science seems to get close in some ways, a grouping of theories that all fit together, but there are other ones that shatter all of those to the ground. But when you see the world as holographic, as consciousness, based on potential and our experiences, suddenly a real theory of everything starts to make perfect sense.

If all in the known universe exists as a wave of potential and requires something to interact with it to make it solid, someone or something to observe it to give it physical form, then perhaps life is more fluid than we were told it to be. And if the very person, the observer, is in fact creating something solid from something fluid, and that observer is creating their physical world from their own experiences, feelings, and thoughts, then what they are seeing, creating and manifesting is directly influenced by all of that.

I could spend an entire book talking about all of the science behind this stuff, but the truth is, I'm not really interested in the science. Some people are, some people really need the FACTS, "Give me the scientific proof damn it!" If that is your bag, feel free to go look, I'm sure you'll find a lot of fascinating stuff out there as I did when I was interested in such things, but for the sake of the book, I'm going to keep it simple as we move on to how this relates to death.

(Now might be a good time to start writing down some of the thoughts coming up for you, or digging deeper into the subjects that I've only breezed over that you find interesting.)

What is Death?

What is death to you? If you are religious and take an afterlife approach, perhaps death is the place your soul goes after your physical body dies on this planet. Or maybe you believe in a place after this life, maybe you think heaven and hell are real and that if you are a good person you'll get into the good place someday. Or maybe you are of a scientific mind, maybe you believe that when we die, our body and being cease to exist, just like my seven year old self thinking that when life ends my body and mind die with it and I am no more. Maybe my body decomposes and turns into something else but life as I know it, my brain and thoughts alike, is over. Or perhaps you believe in karma, or like the Hindu religion, believe that the soul is reincarnated in this life to a new form, either going forward or backwards in the totem of life depending on how your life was lived previously.

I would say in general these are typically the three most popular beliefs about death in most of society, with plenty of variations. But what if there was another version of death, one that was far more simple, one that was not based on faith, religion, or science as much as a clear understanding of what life and reality really is? What might that be like?

Let's say for a moment, for the sake of understanding this concept, that you went into a coma. While you were in that coma you were dreaming rather vivid dreams. You knew you weren't quite awake, but you were stuck in a dream, having a large number of seemingly random experiences. When you woke from that coma, while you may not have much of a clue how long you had been out, you would be aware that there was some movement in time thanks to the dream state you were inhabiting. However, if you went into a coma and had no dreams, had no awareness or consciousness, it would be entirely possible that upon waking up you would perceive that no time had passed, a common thing that happens to people that are comatose. Everyone around you, as well as records, dates, and time, could have been moving 3 years ahead, but if you were in a coma for that long with no awareness, it might feel like a second had gone by. Why is that?

For starters, as Einstein said, time is relative to the observer. If there is no one observing time, they could not perceive the movement of it. If there is no consciousness to perceive the coma, to dream, or to be aware of things going on outside, then it is entirely possible, and rather likely, that you would experience none of the passing time. Meaning that consciousness and awareness are the things that create the concept and feeling that time is passing. Without being aware or awake, you would perceive nothing.

It was when I started thinking about this that it all clicked. Death is only a concept, not something to fear, but more words to abolish. Sure we see people around us dying all of the time, we have friends and loved ones that pass on. We love and miss them, get sad, depressed even, go to their funerals, think about them fondly, tell stories about the good times we shared together, and have our rituals to remember them, but our own death, without us to experience it, is only a concept.

We have our life and our ability to think, feel, taste, smell and all of that, but without any awareness, there is no being to perceive death. Death is just an idea. And sure, if you believe in one of the aforementioned forms of death above; religion, karma, etc., then yes, death is very real, and I am not here to prove you wrong. But if you step outside of that for a second and think about what life really is, consciousness and awareness, and if there is no one to perceive and be aware of life, there is no one to be aware of death, so it cannot be real. It is merely an idea, a concept that we see around us, but that we cannot experience ourselves.

We can make assumptions of what it is like for other people, but we can never know death, just as we can never actually look at ourselves from our own two eyes, only our reflection.

So long as I am conscious, I am. If I know that I am, then I have life. If I don't know that I am, there is no me to perceive what is and what is not. I could wake up tomorrow in a totally different state, my physical body may die and fade away, I may shift into a different reality altogether—one where farts are the most important currency and everyone punches each other in the face as a way to show that they care. But if I am aware of it, if I have consciousness, I still am. The scenario may feel different, it may be the same, or far more or far less pleasant, but if I am aware of it, I still am.

Who is to say that that new place we are in is the afterlife? And who is to say that the place we are in now is the now life? All we have are our ideas about what is and what is not.

This also starts to touch on another sort of death, a very real death that is necessary on the path to awakening—the death of the ego. As humans we perceive life from the perspective of self, the idea that we have a physical body, with our own thoughts, ideas, beliefs, urges, fears, genital sizes, bank accounts and food preferences. But on the path to truth-realization there is one death that is really the ONLY death and the idea of the individual self must die if we are to rid ourselves of ego and the illusion that we are living in.

Yes, we perceive death all around us and it seems so real, but if we are all in fact connected, if we are all truly one piece of something much bigger, then there is no single individual that can die. Maybe their physical presence passes on into a new form of life, but they live on through us, just as we live on through those in our life. To be aware of our life is to have life, and if there is no us to be aware, there is no us to know and experience death. When we lose someone we love it can be soul crushing, but it's also part of the culture that we live in. Many cultures around the world celebrate the physical death as the ultimate death, as the path towards something far bigger and greater, they are not necessarily sad in some cases (which of course there is nothing wrong to be if you are as I have been on many occasions around death), but instead they rejoice and honor the person passing on.

Death doesn't scare me. It used to, and not just when I was a little boy, hoping that my plane would make it to Florida, but throughout most of my adult life. But I like to face all things, even the scariest ones, head on, and thus the only death I have come to know is the death of the ego, the false self. That surely can die. The idea that we are an individual on this planet, that we have this one physical body, that our thoughts are our own, to hold, to fight for, can certainly die and is a big part of what the Buddha describes as being the path to end suffering. For, as he explains, life is transient, ever changing, impermanent, and when we cling and attach ourselves to such things, we suffer. And that clinging on to stuff includes our death and those around us. It may sound harsh or soulless, and is if you look at it from the perspective of ego, but when the ego is dead, it's nothing really special at all, it just is.

What I find most incredibly interesting about consciousness is our ability to shift it the more clear we get. You hear about manifestation all of the time yet it can seem so far fetched. But if we are not actually physical beings, but beings existing in a wave of potential, creating an external solid reality wherever we go, then it is entirely possible that our internal world really reflects our external world. That all ideas, thoughts and concepts come from within and show up as an external reality. That even death, in the most physical ways, is only based around our perception and understanding of what we believe it to be.

Imagine for a second that our eyes do not take in light but instead project the world around us, like a projector displaying a movie. The classical way of looking at the world is that our senses take in what is outside of us and our brain interprets it, but what if they really project the world into existence? Things can seem so random and chaotic when we believe we are one small individual in a sea of billions, or one small planet in an ocean of infinity, but when we begin to realize that the universe is really a part of us, that we are as much inside the universe as it is outside of us, then the illusion that we are separate slowly begins to melt away.

In time we see that we are not a single organism fighting for survival, but instead we make up all of existence, every piece of us holds all of the knowledge in the universe and in seeing and knowing this we can unlock it. Call it holographic, call it God or consciousness, call it enlightenment or unity, wherever you look, when you strip away all of the confusion, it's staring you right in the face.

By having this understanding of the world, suddenly things aren't so dark, grim, and isolating, suddenly we are the people we meet, we are everything that we see, we are one with the universe and the universe is one with us. It is easy to see separation, and the ego wants to hold on to the idea that we are an individual, that we are floating in a sea of nothingness, trying our best to get by and be as successful and happy as we can. But we can step back and realize we are not separate, that we exist as a wave of potential, and while we may be living in a world that feels isolating and wrong in many ways, it is through our own inner action and unshaken knowing that we can shift our internal world and reflect a new external world, one of truth, connection, and seeing what is and what is not.

As we continue this conversation, feel free to start playing around with these concepts in your life. Imagine perhaps that you are not as separate as you once thought. Also know that while we continue I will be referring to my past experiences throughout the book, and use the term "I" quite often and so "I" invite you to see what it might feel like reading as though the "I" that is speaking isn't really "me" at all but a potential "thing" that can allow you to experience something new and deconstruct your life to get you closer to seeing the truth of who "you" are. When I killed off the ego, when I experienced the one and only true death, suddenly all my fears and confusion around death ceased to exist.

Death may be very real to you, or as you deconstruct it you may begin to see that it is no more than a concept, a word, an idea to keep you on your toes, keep you guessing, searching, wondering, hoping, or even fearing. I see nothing wrong with having a framework for the afterlife if it makes you feel better and gives you hope and a reason to be a good person in this life, or heck gives you a reason to give it all you've got because you think this is the only life, then by all means, go for it. However, if you've been struggling with death, fearing it, confused in an endless sea of nothingness, start to realize that the YOU that you are so afraid of dying is no more than the false-self, the ego, the separate self that must die in order to see the truth of what is. The same goes for other people in your life, if you fear their death or are still struggling with their passing, being sad and grieving are all very real and valuable processes, but if you are still stuck in the "why did this happen to them," phase, start to look at where the question is really coming from.

This feels like a good time to add in a short piece on consciousness that I love and am constantly in awe of. This waking life that we exist in, as I have been sharing about, seems very real, and in its "realness" it is easy to make assumptions about what is not real. We watch movies about witches and wizards, intergalactic alien wars and beyond and for the most part know them to be fiction because we are so sure that the other stuff is not. But there isn't anything that I see as more or less real in the world, not magic, not aliens, not men made of mangoes.

It is all just as real and possible as it is not. I make no distinction between the magic I read about in a Harry Potter book and the magic that moves my fingers as they write these words. It's all magic and when you dissolve the ego you start to realize that the magic that makes up our universe is far more exciting and vast than all the stuff we have seen and read about in fairytales.

I share this last point in this chapter for those that want to step in to a movie like Harry Potter and so wish that Hogwarts really does exist so that they could experience all of the spells and potions and fantastic beasts. While that stuff may be fantasy and fiction written by a creative genius, it doesn't mean there isn't magic that is far more potent in this world.

Maybe we can't fly on a magic broom stick, or maybe we can, who knows what you do with the rest of your existence in this dimension or another, but the first step is always destroying what is not so that you can start to experience what is, and what that is you can't even begin to imagine until you can. So stop debating what may and may not be real and start actually taking a look and you just might see that your whole life is alive with magic already.

My Near Death Experience

I shared the story about being hit by a car and nearly dying for a few reasons, but felt like they would make a heck of a lot more sense after explaining my experience with death, so now I will leave you with a few final thoughts to ponder.

I never really knew what happened the day of the accident. I used to wonder if I did actually die in some fashion and that this new life I am in now is really the "afterlife" or some alternate timeline, but as I've come to express from a consciousness perspective, it's just another belief. It makes me think of all of the stories of people that have near death experiences and how often times they report nearing a tunnel with white light, or going out of their body and being able to see everything that is happening, or speaking to some sort of ascended master or God like being.

Whatever it may be, what really stands out has stayed constant since I started seeing death in a new light. Even if someone experiences a near death experience there is still a consciousness aware of the experience. Maybe their entire life flashes before their very eyes, or they perceive that their soul floated above their body and that they could see themselves being operated on in a hospital bed. Some even claim to come back with heightened abilities or magic powers. All very exciting and even convincing at times, but still all from the perspective of consciousness. It may not be the same type of experience we usually endure in life, but if you have a memory of it, are aware of it, then what makes it all that different from anything else, whether it be during meditation, a drug induced hallucination, a dream or waking life? Why must we assume that this life is THE real life and the others are not?

So many people like to spend time pondering altered states of consciousness, which can be fun to think about, and even more fun to actually do, but it is still consciousness and who's to say that one is more real, or more great or more anything than another? I could wake up from this life right now, the one I've lived for 34 years only to find out that it was no more than a dream. Have you ever had a dream that you were so sure was real while you were in it? Maybe for just a moment, or maybe it felt like it was forever, but convincing nonetheless. And so long as it is in the scope of consciousness, it is still part of all that is, no matter how we try to philosophize the experience.

And for another thing if I had to guess I think the day of my accident was the day that I died, well, rather a part of my ego died, or at the very least some of the walls it was constructed of. I didn't fully know it then but I have come to see that perhaps the car crash allowed me to step outside of my conditioned body, break my programming, and shift into a new level of understanding and that it simply took many years of being an outsider, never quite fitting in, to finally understand what the point of it all was. That point may be in part writing this book, sharing these stories, connecting with the people in my life, but whatever it is, I no longer fall for death because the only part of me that could ever die is already dead.

Six

On Lying, Truth and Honesty

Lie:

An intentionally false statement

Truth:

The quality or state of being true

Throughout the majority of my life I never considered myself someone who told lies. I spent most of my life priding myself on being honest, and more importantly being someone that people could confide in, share their deepest and darkest secrets with, and feel safe knowing that they wouldn't be judged and that I wouldn't be a blabber mouth. For years and years I even fooled myself into thinking I was telling the truth to myself, but when I started doing some hard digging, it became clear, I was a BIG fuggin liar.

Come to think of it I remember even believing as a child that I invented the phrase; "Liar Liar pants on fire," go figure...

I had spent so much energy creating a safe space where other people felt comfortable to be honest with me, but deep down I was too afraid to be honest with other people, to share what was really going on with me, because I feared what they might say. I suppose you could say I told white lies, I hid things from people that I thought would hurt them or they wouldn't understand. In my head I told myself that it was okay, that I was only trying to protect the people I cared about. I was hiding certain truths, but I wasn't lying, just sheltering them from pain, right? Uh, yeah, fat chance.

This became something I got really good at, telling people what they wanted to hear and believing that I was doing something positive because of it. You know the classic scenario, your partner tries on a dress and asks if it makes them look fat and no matter what you think you say, "No, of course not dear, you look great!". I was doing that in so many areas in my life. In some ways I did feel justified, felt like it wasn't my place to share certain things, like how I knew why my one friend broke up with my other friend. I couldn't tell her, I thought it would destroy her, but I also felt really guilty and stuck in a rough place. And yes, while there is a time and a place and a way to share sensitive information, and some things may be better left unsaid, it was hurting me and those around me in more ways than I could imagine, even though I didn't realize it yet.

As time went on I got better and better at hiding the truth, but I also dug myself into a bigger hole. This harmed me in more ways than one. I found that while I had a lot of people in my life who trusted me, people that felt comfortable sharing their secrets with me, I hardly had anyone in my life that I could be honest with in all of the ways I truly wanted to be. I had dug myself such a big hole that even though I felt like I had all of these close relationships, they were often very one-sided and I struggled to understand why.

It wasn't that the people on the other side weren't trustworthy, just that I created this outside appearance that I didn't need any help, that everything was okay, so people didn't even think I needed someone to confide in. But I was only hiding myself, I was hiding my life when my relationships were failing, when I was struggling with my parents, my band, my health, I hid it all and pretended like everything was okay. Don't want to be a burden on anyone right? Again, wrong!

This went on for years and years. I did a lot of personal development work and slowly started to uncover different elements of myself that I needed to work on, but I had gotten so good at lying that I didn't see just how much I was lying to myself. No matter what self-help books I read, what therapists I went to, I seemed to fall back into the same patterns and had no idea why. I started to see a very destructive pattern that was happening, especially in the moments when it felt so automatic.

The more I dug, the more I started to see how lying to someone else was really just lying to myself. It's easy to think that you can get away with a lie, or do it for the good of the other person, as a way for protection, but knowing that I am connected to everyone around me, and that all my actions have direct outcomes, not being truthful hurts myself too. I am really just lying to myself.

There are so many forms of lies that we tell ourselves, and a big reason I share so much about the importance of looking deep into yourself is not just to work on the pieces that you are aware of, but to see your blind spots and recognize how they have been fooling you. The lies we tell ourselves, the lies we were conditioned to believe from a young age, though we may not be responsible for why they are there, are within our power and responsibility to change.

I kept searching deeper and deeper, looking to excavate anything that was keeping me in this destructive pattern, but then, as if I had no control over it, something intervened and changed my life forever.

A New Beginning to this Story

I find it a little bit comical, if not odd to write a chapter about lying some 100 pages into a book about truth. At this point you may be wondering if everything I have said up until this point is a lie, which of course could possibly be true, but as I have expressed early on, it doesn't so much matter about what is true or untrue so long as you examine it for yourself. A hundred pages in and I still don't feel any need to convince you of anything, and that would be a silly thing to try and do.

After seven wild and wonderful yet equally challenging and confronting years with my partner, we had hit a really hard place and decided in May of 2019 to separate from one another and take some space for a few months. I had just sold my half of Brothers Green Eats to my brother Mike and was in New York City when I started feeling a calling to travel. For the first time in awhile I didn't have anywhere to be for nearly a month and felt a calling to travel to a distant place and do some deep healing work.

Rather quickly it became clear that Peru was the place to go, and while I had no plan and knew little to nothing about Peru, I booked a ticket for two days later in full trust of what was to come. The moment I made the decision and started telling friends, everything clicked into place and my journey was becoming clear. It was settled—I would spend the first portion of the trip in Cusco and the Sacred Valley, experiencing the magic of the Andes and Wachuma, also known as San Pedro, a powerful healing medicine said to be the spirit of the Grandfather. After that I would head into the jungle to meet the Grandmother Spirit, Ayahuasca, an extremely potent psychedelic plant medicine that I had been searching out and fascinated with for nearly ten years but until that point had not felt I was ready for. With a loose plan in place, I packed the last of my things, said goodbye to some friends and was on my way to what would be my first real extended solo backpacking trip.

The Wachuma ceremonies in the Sacred Valley were quite beautiful. I saw within myself a little boy who did not get the love he truly felt he needed growing up, and I saw the man inside of me being able to comfort the boy, protecting him, warming him, keeping him safe, allowing him to breath and grow. I received a message that said; *how can you love someone else if you can't first truly love yourself?* It hit me right in the gut.

So much of my life had been based around trying to please other people. I always felt like half people pleaser, half rebel, when one got to be too much the other would come out and smash the glass house down. But it wasn't necessarily a healthy balance, and so much of my energy and effort went in to doing things for other people, out of the good of my heart sure, maybe, but also out of a deep desire to feel loved and needed, not able to face what I might feel if I spoke my own truth at the risk of disturbing the peace.

The day after my second ceremony in the Andes I walked by a large flock of playful school children, prancing down the street, laughing gleefully, entirely immersed in the moment. Upon seeing such a sight, I immediately felt envy, lack, loss, need, wanting to be in a light and silly state, filled with joy, as the children I saw were. And then I was reminded of another message I had received the day before—their joy is my joy, their laughter is my laughter, I am not separate from it, but a part of it all.

Immediately I felt lightness and relief. It was in these moments that I often found myself almost automatically going to separation, it is the way in which I had always been programmed. But through the various stages of awareness, the more I explored the vastness of myself, the more I aligned with my deep connection to all. Something about speaking my truth was starting to unravel but I wasn't sure what.

After the sacred valley, I found myself traveling deep into the jungle to do my first Ayahuasca ceremony with a Curandera (a medicine woman not unlike a Shaman). Everything lined up perfectly. I was put in touch with a powerful plant medicine healer that would take me to a special part of the jungle and facilitate a one-on-one Ayahuasca plant ceremony retreat for me for one week. I didn't know what to expect, but it felt like the right time, the calling was knocking and I had no doubt I was ready to respond.

I met Mesa, my Curandera, in a jungle town called Tarapoto before heading off to where we would be holding ceremony. What makes Tarapoto unique is that it is where the mountains meet the jungle, so it is still hot and lush and green, but it isn't as intense and thick and humid as the deep jungle. The weather is a little more mild and the views are breathtaking. From there we drove about an hour to a small town known for its Cacao production called Chazuta.

We stayed overnight, and she bought all of the necessary things we needed; food, water and other supplies, then early the next morning we hiked about an hour into the jungle, crossing nearly waist high rivers, with what seemed like no end in sight, a donkey carrying the heavy load of our stuff.

When we finally arrived I was stunned by what I saw: cacao trees as far as the eye could see, coconuts, bananas, lush green hillsides, and a collection of small huts made of wood and basic materials from the jungle. The structures had no walls, just a roof and four posts holding them up.

One was covering a rustic wooden dining table, another, with a collection of hammocks, housed a very basic kitchen where everything we ate would be cooked over fire, and four similar structures where guests would bunk.

My hut was a short walk from the kitchen and a little closer to the bathroom. There was no shower but there was one toilet that flushed with a sheet to cover for privacy. I unpacked my things and noticed my sleeping arrangements were unlike anything I had experienced before. It consisted of a small wooden platform with a thin cheap mattress, a mosquito net to keep the bugs out, and a basic wood and dried leaf covering over my head, but no walls.

Things didn't become fully real until I was given a cup of tobacco juice to drink, along with a ton of water, that was supposed to help me purge and cleanse my body before our first ceremony the following night. I hate tobacco, never liked smoking it, nor smelling it, so drinking a cup felt a little bit, alright a lot bit, torturous as it burned all the way down, but I was there to go full in and I knew there was no way around it. At that point I was supposed to immediately start throwing up, only I didn't and started to get worried.

Mesa told me that I was holding on too tight, that I needed to relax and should try and take a nap. When I awoke an hour or so later I felt extremely dizzy and nauseous, jumped out of bed, grabbed my puke bucket, and purged my face off, expelling all that was inside of me, opening up for what was to come.

The first night was extremely mild and I hardly felt the medicine at all, but I knew in my bones that it was building up to something and I needed only to be patient. The next day we prepared for another ceremony. The foods Mesa made were very simple; rice, lentils, some boiled vegetables, hardly any salt or seasoning, no oils, just the most basic of things plus a few fruits from the jungle. I bathed in the river as the little minnows nipped away at my legs, walked around the property picking fresh cacao fruit (which is absolutely out of this world), and mostly just sat in a hammock, staring into the lush green jungle, totally present.

After only a few days of being there I was already noticing a huge shift in my focus. Finding that back home I was so engrossed in my phone, the fact that my job was basically to be on social media didn't help, and I began to notice how bored I often got, scrolling through my phone, looking for something to spark a moment of joy in me. But here I was—totally present, no internet service, no technology, just immersed in the jungle. I could stare at a tree for hours and be totally content.

That day Mesa and I spoke about the first ceremony. She felt that I was being a bit uptight, holding on instead of letting go and relaxing, that inside I wanted to control my journey instead of giving myself over to it. I was starting to see the link between my need to people please, hide the truth, and control. I always saw myself as a "go with the flow" type person, which was true in many ways, but deep down I desperately wanted to control the outcome of any situation I was in, control what people thought of me, how they interacted with me, all because I was afraid, I just didn't really know why I couldn't drop the act.

The second ceremony was more powerful than the first but still relatively mild. This time however I felt the medicine working through me, having gone right for a full cup (about a shot glass worth as her medicine was quite strong). I didn't purge, but I did feel it pulsing through my veins as she sang her medicine songs, weaving a tapestry of magic through my being, like a hummingbird flying through every crevice of my insides.

I felt the medicine in me and I could feel my body, I was uncomfortable, trying my best to sit up against the wall and adjust, but I kept moving around in my discomfort. I saw a vision of myself as a child, alone in a crib, scared and lonely. I saw that I did not have the love and warmth from my mother that I imagined most children had and that I, as a grown adult, had to give that love to my inner child, rock and comfort them, to reawaken the dance in that child.

After a few hours of this I ended up lying down on my back and started physically rocking myself up and down on the ground as Mesa sang her sweet medicine songs that were like lullabies comforting my child within. I felt so much joy and love, my smile was practically ripping through my face. It was wonderful. The medicine was stronger the second time around but I still noticed that I was working with it in a sense, that I hadn't given myself fully to it, still allowing Mother Ayahuasca to do her work almost as if under my supervision or support.

That night, while I was still on the medicine but not as intensely as during the ceremony, Mesa walked me back to my hut in the pitch dark. On the way back to my hut I looked up and noticed the stars. They nearly took my breath away, I felt like I could almost reach out and grab them, hundreds of trillions of stars, all crystal clear, right within my grasp. I got in bed, recorded a little video of my experience on my GoPro, and quickly fell asleep. When I woke up an hour later I could hardly comprehend and believe what was happening.

Ayahuasca and the Earthquake

As my eyes tried to open, it was pitch dark and I could hardly tell whether I was really awake or not, still feeling the effects of Ayahuasca. I grabbed my phone and turned on the light to find that my entire hut was shaking vigorously back and forth. I went from confusion to panic as I tried to piece together what was going on and whether it was really happening or not. As I slowly began to settle into the intense yet rhythmic rocking motion of my entire hut and bed, which in some ways felt like an extension of my medicine ceremony just hours before, I started to turn my panic into curiosity, which ultimately led to trust as I rode out the final moments in total surrender.

When everything settled I managed to fall back asleep rather quickly, not even really thinking to leave my hut and check in with Mesa. The next morning I awoke to find out that an 8.5 earthquake that lasted around 45 seconds had hit with its epicenter being close to where we were staying. Though there may have been damage outside of where we were staying, everything on the property was completely okay. We had no real way of talking to the outside world and I wondered if Jaquy might be worried, but I did my best to tune in and send trusting signals her way.

If that wasn't enough of a powerful sign, I would also come to find out that the beloved medicine man that built the property we were staying on and had hosted so many people like myself on his sacred land, assisting them in plant ceremonies, came to pass away that very night. It was sad for everyone connected to his wonderful presence in life, and almost as if his passing had truly rocked the world, which it may certainly have. Mesa and I spoke about whether to leave the jungle and go back early but ultimately she decided he would have wanted us to continue the work as it was so important to him.

We took the night off and the following day I prepared for our final medicine ceremony, bathing myself in a special herbal blend Mesa had made before and slowly preparing for what I knew would be a powerful night.

Awaken the inner child,
nurture him o' sweet music and medicine.
The scared boy who just wanted love,
Yet received fear, anger and hate in its place.
Go to that precious soul,
see him,
hold him,
lift him,
love him,
remind him that he can heal,
that he can live in love.
That he can live his truth,
that he is deserving and worthy,
worthy to live in a life outside of this pain and fear, and that it does not
have to be his story,
That it is only HIStory.

-Yoshua

Leading up to the final ceremony I was processing a lot, as one might imagine. A big theme that continued to come up was the grip I not only had on my life, but on the ceremonies in general. It seemed as though I was able to feel the plant medicine in my body but didn't have enough trust to fully give myself over to the medicine, to Mother Ayahuasca. Perhaps my own lack of trust with my own mother, or perhaps there was another reason. Regardless, I wanted so badly to trust myself, to remember what it felt like to surrender to the universe and integrate with its oneness. I had been lost for many years and no matter what I did, I couldn't shake the feeling. I had come to see complete truth in the universe years before but for some reason was still holding on to fear no matter what I did.

That night when I got to the ceremony I felt open and ready in a way I had not the two ceremonies before. As I drank I finally felt ready to surrender and I was in full trust, ready for what may come. And when it did come, I saw everything. I could write for pages and pages about what came next—my being rocketing up into what felt like her magic kingdom of light and love, the sacred information I was given as Mother Ayahuasca took over every inch of my being, bringing me into her all-knowing embrace, sharing with me details about friendships and loved ones I had not seen before, exposing me to certain hidden truths about different aspects of nature, plants, insects and our connection to it all.

How suddenly, once the medicine kicked in, when most nights I could still feel a me with a physical body in the room working alongside the plant, now there was no me, and I had no body. I could share about how I went into the deepest, darkest, scariest and most fear based visions and right as I was starting to freak out, remembered to trust, and in doing so integrated with everything that ever was, outside of judgment and assumptions. I could try my best to capture in words what was nearly impossible to even comprehend in feelings, but it wasn't so much about the experience that rocked my world but rather what came next because of it.

I had finally gotten to a space of total trust within myself to let the medicine do its work on me. I didn't throw up that night, but I did back purge as they call it and when the strongest of the effects finally did wear off, I found myself going to the toilet every few minutes and clearing what felt like childhood lifetimes of eating terrible food. Even though my diet had been good for many years, it felt like my body was doing a deep cleaning the likes of which I had never experienced, like I had drank a bottle of "safe for human consumption" drano.

I had fully surrendered and was finally blessed with the perfect wisdom and intelligence of Mother Ayahuasca. I had done other psychedelic medicines before but there was something about this that was different. I truly felt an intelligent mother like presence with me the entire time, guiding me, showing me all that I needed to see.

The next day I spent my time in the jungle alone. Mesa went back to town to check on the arrangements for the funeral and trusted me to watch over the sacred land on my own. I spent the day relaxing, reflecting, and capturing what I remembered from the night before. When she later returned and we spoke of the ceremony I was amazed just how in tune she was with me. As she sang her medicine songs each night, I didn't fully comprehend just how connected she was to my experience until she recollected almost entirely what I was going through in each moment, even though it was pitch dark and I didn't share anything.

We spoke about the ceremony, and the importance of the medicine, and how with the popularity of Ayahuasca there have been increasingly more troubling stories and bad practices, and how important it was to educate people on the truth of the plants. Of course we also spoke about my need to be honest with myself, share what I knew to be true, not get so wrapped up in my codependency in my relationship, and give myself more space to feel and trust.

When I returned home I didn't quite feel like the ceremonies and my experience in Peru had healed me completely. It felt more like a clearing, as if the work I had done in the jungle really just opened something up and that upon returning to my home the real work was going to begin. I was right in ways I could not have imagined.

Busting Open the Flood Gates

When I returned home it was quite a shift to try and integrate back into my life. In the jungle I felt so present and I loved being away from social media and the internet. While I missed my friends and family, I also felt at peace and was slightly concerned of what might start to fade when I plugged myself back into life. Jaquy and I had a series of long conversations and decided, to both of our delight, that we wanted to be together and work things out.

A few months went by and slowly some of the struggles we were having started to creep back in. One day I did a mushroom ceremony as I knew, under the right circumstances, hallucinogenic mushrooms could be a great healing tool and a way to deepen my integration process back home. I had done my fair share of mushroom journeys in the past, but I felt like I was armed with new tools and wisdom to go deeper than I ever had before.

Things were starting out quite lovely and light at first, but a few hours in I had this deep urge to have my solar plexus touched by her hand. The second it happened I burst out crying uncontrollably, screaming, laughing, balling my eyes out, tears streaming down my cheeks. It went on for what felt like 30 minutes. As someone that rarely cries and struggles to really let go in this way, it was a huge breakthrough. I had never been so hysterical in my life.

It was in that moment that something unlocked in me, something that Ayahuasca had pointed towards, but perhaps felt I wasn't ready to see yet. I saw visions of myself as a child, quite young, that I had held on to. I discovered and saw that I had repressed some sexual trauma and abuse at a young age and buried it deep down. But in that moment I saw it all and a giant portal of truth had been unlocked deep within me.

It was hard to relive that moment from my childhood, and what exactly happened is still not completely clear, but I knew something had happened, perhaps many times even, and that I had locked it away deep deep down. But things were different now, I was no longer a helpless child, and I could go into those old hidden memories and face them head on, confront the moment, reframing it, and start the healing process which I had avoided for so long.

It would be a short time after that in a somatic therapy session that I would say the words "I don't know what I am sexually," where I would continue to further my path towards truth. You see, as I spoke of the pursuit of digging deep into yourself to get to the bottom of who you really are, I had missed a key point to all of this. Yes, knowledge is extremely valuable, having a clear grip on what is true and what is untrue is powerful, but our body has such a deep rooted wisdom that stems far beyond our minds ability to think and process. You might call it higher mind or whatever feels right, but the thinking mind is really just the first step.

In somatic or body based therapy it is believed that traumatic experiences are stored in the body and if we only talk through our experiences and thoughts, though we can conceptualize who we are and why we do what we do, we can't necessarily fully embody the changes we are thinking about. To do that we have to feel them in our body, hence the importance of em-BODYing things.

The body holds trauma, aka fear, and often these fears shape our life and our decisions, even more than the ones in our mind, like a thin veil of falseness forcing our every decision. I had repressed such deep pain and spent the majority of my life trying to hide from it, doing anything to avoid a situation where I might have to feel that pain again and bring it to the surface.

I could say I was lying to myself, but as one of my best friends Clay put it, "I don't think you are lying to yourself, it sounds more like you are just uncovering new layers of truth about who you really are". Whichever way one might look at it, my life changed drastically in that moment. I saw why it was so hard for me to express how I really felt to others, why I felt I needed to control things so much. I couldn't risk the pain, it was unbearable, and so I subconsciously repressed it rather than allowing it to come to the surface.

Before I get into the realizations, and since I don't have a

specific chapter about this in my book, I wanted to briefly make note of what I have called "plant medicine" on more than one occasion in this book. I want to make it very clear that doing this deeper work does not have to look like going to the jungle, or eating a handful of mushrooms in a ceremonial space. The plants can assist you to go deep if they call to you, but I know plenty of people who have done powerful healing work without the assistance of plant medicine or hallucinogenic drugs.

I bring this up because I don't want you to assume that the work I talk about in this book has to go hand in hand with anything other than yourself. Maybe you get outside help, a coach, a therapist, a mantra, but whatever you do, do it well and trust that your intuition will guide you and lead the way to uncover whatever it is you have to uncover. I've developed a healthy relationship with plant medicine, but I have also gone just as deep and uncovered just as much in a completely sober state. There is no one right way, just so long as you do it your way and feel good about it. Anyhow, back to the story.

When all of this broke open in my life I was finally able to

look at some of the bigger things that I always ran from. The moment I said out loud in my hypnotic state that I didn't know what my sexuality was I saw that I had always had attractions to both men and women but never allowed myself to explore the attractions to men because it was too painful—the moment the thoughts came up, I pushed them down and distracted myself. I saw the same with my gender and sexuality.

Growing up I always felt like I had a strong feminine side but I never really allowed myself to look at the fact that I felt as much a woman inside as I did a man, always feeling sort of in-between the two with no clear definite side to choose other than the biological one. I never gave myself the space to look because it seemed too painful, too confusing, too scary to face. My conditioning and my trauma were working together hand in hand.

With the floodgates of truth open, my sexuality washed over me like a tidal wave. I had allowed myself to fully experience and relive the sexual trauma I experienced as a kid and was able to process it as an adult so that it no longer controlled me. Everything that I struggled to make sense of before suddenly started to come into total clarity.

After a few days of processing I spoke openly and honestly with Jaquy about what this meant for me and for us. After hours upon hours of conversation I made the hardest choice in my life—to leave my marriage. As much as I so deeply loved her, so badly wanted our life to work out as we had seen possible, I knew I had been living a lie. I knew that our lives were going in different directions and that I needed to see what life was like when I lived in my full truth on my own.

It was the scariest thing I had ever done, but it was also the first time I could truly be honest with every fibre of my being. I did everything I could to make our marriage work, we both did, but we had grown apart, and I was no longer afraid to let go of something that wasn't working, no matter how wonderful she is and how much I loved her and she loved me.

How do you define yourself?

Having just exploded open my life, I initially felt pressured to define myself, to put a label on who I was to make it clear to people. Was I bisexual? Queer? Or was I a transgender in some way? Was I gender fluid? Non-binary? With so many new words and pronouns flooding to the surface of our culture, I struggled to find one that defined me. I had family come in town just a week after all of this went down and I tried my best to explain it to them with little avail. And then, once I finally had room to breathe, it hit me like a ton of bricks. Truth trumps all...

It wasn't about trying to label myself, breaking out of one box only to put myself in another, no, it was about me living in my truth. I didn't need a label, call me what you will, I simply am. What mattered was that I could now finally live life in truth, not in fear and hiding, but as the fullest expression of myself. It had felt like my whole life there was this thin layer or fear surrounding me that I was completely blind to, shaping and guiding me, and once it was gone, I was free.

I had tried so hard to fit into being some version of the definition of a straight male in my relationship and as much as I tried to make it work and be who I thought I had to be, it didn't align with who I truly was. Having now seen who I really was, I knew, without a shred of doubt, that I could not go on pretending, no matter how hard and scary it was to think about.

For 34 years I had lived my life in a deep state of repressed fear and now, for the first time in my life, I let myself explore what it meant, not physically, but mentally, to let my mind go wherever it needed to go, with no blocks or judgments for where it went. My early childhood traumas created a space where I never felt safe exploring and seeing who I was. It was too scary to explore the parts of me that I buried deep down. And so I hid a big part of myself not only from everyone close to me, but also from myself. I locked it deep away and did anything to create a false narrative to justify who I felt that I had to be, but it was just another costume, another character to try and make sense of the world.

These realizations have sent me on a powerful journey, one that has been the scariest, but also most relieving, freeing and honest one. Losing my partner both crushed my heart and dampened my spirit and has tested me in ways that I have never even thought possible. In all of our years together I did everything to avoid hurting or upsetting Jaquy but I also saw that ultimately I was living a lie and that was fair to no one.

You can't know what you don't know until one day you do. For me it became abundantly clear that I spent most of my life creating codependent relationships and friendships as a way to try and get something that I now know I can never get from an external source. I just wanted to be loved and instead of dealing with my trauma and creating a space where I could be and see who I was beyond the character, I did everything that I could to be what I thought I needed to be to make others happy, while actively repressing my pain. And in doing so I wasn't living in truth, which hurt me and the people I loved more than I ever intended.

It still pains me sometimes to think about, as a loss on any level can create all sorts of grief, but when I get beyond my own hurt and judgment against myself, I see nothing but clarity, growth, love and appreciation for all of the relationships in my life. Our life together was one of the best adventures that I have ever experienced in my entire life, as challenging as it was at times, I would not change a single thing. Now I am on a new adventure and I have nothing but gratitude for the one that came before.

Fluid and Flowing

Everyone seems to have things and parts of themselves that they hide or push down out of fear of judgment, fear of failure, disappointment, banishment and in some cases far scarier potential outcomes. But the more I live from a place of truth, the more life starts to feel like a picture instead of a puzzle made up of a bunch of different shaped pieces that I'm trying to frantically place together.

I feel light because I am finally free from my emotional prison of untruth. I am living from my feelings, connected to what is, not what fear tells me must be. And I write and share this with you, the honest nature of myself, because the old ways, the paradigm of one or the other, male or female, this or that, wrong or right, the dualistic nature of choices, is gone. Like a sweet fart in the wind, the uncomfortable gas I was holding on to in my stomach, painfully keeping me in check, has all blown away.

When we consider ourselves to be one thing, it can feel safe to condense that thing to a label, seeing the other contrasting side as different, and while doing so feeling a sense of comfort in the things that we are. If that works for you, keep on a workin it, but if you feel like something isn't right, keep digging deeper. We are fluid and flowing individuals sharing as much uniqueness as similarities, and when we break the box of what we are supposed to be, what a man or woman is meant to dress like, talk like, do, think or feel, we allow what is to come through and our being integrates harmoniously with the world around us. We tune into the frequency and suddenly it all becomes clear. We are who we are, not who the label says we are, but who we know ourselves to truly be.

Ayahuasca: a post mini-memoir

Upon returning home from my second set of Ayahuasca ceremonies I have been reflecting on the experiences, and while I had a lot of great insight, there is only one thing that I feel is worth sharing. These ceremonies were quite different from my first; no purging, no darkness, no giant visions, instead only clarity. Sure I had some moments that were sad, reflecting on and grieving the end of my marriage, really going into the feelings and the loss that I had experienced, allowing myself to process such things, but from a state of love and clarity.

But what happened that I didn't expect was what I am really here to share. Ayahuasca, as I have come to see it, is a very powerful plant medicine that plays into your fears, hopes, desires, worldview, all of your consciousness, to create a story of sorts, almost like a virtual movie for you to experience as a way to show you things and help you move past blocks and uncover fears and trauma.

For some people, this is a really visual experience, a symbolic one even —being shown great animal spirits and protectors, given energetic weapons to fight off demons, being transformed into intergalactic beings. For others it is much more physical, purging the things that are inside that we hold onto, letting them go through the act of throwing up, shaking, crying, sweating, yelling, and so on and so forth. But Ayahuasca has no assumptions when you don't go into it with any, even if most people do.

My first experiences were all sorts of things, I had the metaphors, symbols, the transforming into animals and being shown sacred teachings, and all of that. But then I went home, integrated it all into my life, made gigantic major changes, and continued on with my life from this new space. So my second time around during a plant medicine retreat, which wasn't something I had planned but rather been hired to assist and teach at, things were quite different.

In my most recent ceremonies most of what I felt was really pleasant, I had no grand visions, I had things I worked through, but I mostly just felt clear, felt aware, felt present and felt the medicine dancing through my body. A lot of my ceremonies felt more like a celebration, like the mask had been dropped, like the visual story that played on my screen was gone, the veil had been lifted, and I simply experienced the beautiful nothingness that I had covered up for so long.

If you do any sort of deep healing work, especially around plants, don't simply go home, not take action, slowly forget about it as you fall back into your normal life, and then feel like you have to go back again to do it all over (I've seen it a hundred times...). Implement the teachings, go into what you saw with an open mind, make the changes you know you can't avoid, lean in to the fear, and as you continue to move forward you just might find that that work is done. Who knows, maybe it's not forever, maybe it is, but for now you can drop the story and see how it feels to be free of it all.

Seven

On Food, Music and the Physical Stuff

Most of this book, in one way or another, pertains to a recognizing of the false-self and a disarming of that character, piece by piece, in order to connect to something within you that is much more expansive. While a lot of that journey may seem to exist within the thinking mind, since the mind and body are completely connected, there are a lot of physical things that you can do that are great ways to get out of the mind, almost as if to lose your mind just a little bit (or completely), in order to see what lies beyond.

I decided to dedicate most of my experience with food and music to another book within the same series, but I felt it best to include at least a small part of why, for me, these energies have been two of the most important in my life. I'm not using these examples to say that they are necessary or the ultimate ways to get in touch with the physical, there are so many different forms of movement, connection exercises, rituals, sports, practices and such that I have done and gotten a lot out of, and many more that I have not, that may work for you. However, as music and food are at the center of almost every single culture in the known world to some degree, I see them as fundamental human things that anyone can develop a personal relationship with.

I want to share a bit about music and food from the energetic standpoint, using them both as vehicles to tap into certain parts of ourselves that may be laying dormant; to access our creativity, to take a risk, try something new, build human connection, heal and nourish ourselves, and the like. Whether you've been a musician your whole life or never played a note, or are a famous chef or never picked up a knife, it doesn't really matter so long as your mind is open.

"When we dance, we wake up, we get down and juicy with ourselves, we have fun and forget all the heavy shit we carry around. In the dance we get real, get free, get over ourselves. Movement kicks ass."

— *Gabrielle Roth, Connections: The Threads of Intuitive Wisdom*

Music is, without a doubt, my first language, English a distant second. If I would have to guess I'd say I'm mostly made up of music, with a hint of human in there doing its best to hold on to its form just enough to get by and function in the "normal" world. To get a better sense of what I am speaking about, you need only look to music and what it represents in the world. I'm not necessarily speaking about a specific style of music, whether it be popular music, classical music, funk, reggae, even polka, I make no distinction between styles.

A song that makes me feel something, that moves me, both emotionally and or physically, is a wonderful thing that can unravel hidden layers deep within me that my thinking mind might otherwise miss. There are so many musicians and bands that have had a drastic impact on my life, and I am grateful for popular music of a wide variety of styles, and yet, when I speak of music, I speak of its essence, which goes far beyond a structured song, and the most basic fabric of vibration permeating through all of existence.

Music is the universal language, the language of love, the language of life, because it is all. When we tune in to these essential frequencies we are reminded that we are one with everything. The rhythm of the universe is always there, it never goes away, we need only to catch its infinite wave and ride with it, flow with it. Everyone is made of music, you are a musician through and through, if you have a heartbeat you have rhythm, a voice (even if only an internal one), a song.

Bands can channel truth in their music, musicians can tap into universal knowledge, a human can eat a bunch of acid and experience godhood or oneness with all, but most humans are still, in their everyday state, confined by ego. A musician may be able to tap in to a deeper state of consciousness, and create incredible music to help you get there, but to assume that that person lives in that state in their everyday existence is often only another distraction keeping you feeling separate from the pure essence of it all. I've read enough band biographies to know just how much the ego can get in the way and destroy so many great bands no matter what their intentions might be.

Ownership of music is an interesting thing. From the most basic vibrational level, no one can have any true ownership over music, just like no one can truly have ownership over another person or a piece of nature. As the catalyst of the experience, sure, musicians can make money from it, having a career in such a vast art form makes perfect sense and can be quite lovely, besides everyone has gotta eat. Even though your favorite band can be a great channel to share incredible music with you, no one owns the ability to make you feel something through vibration, that feeling is a universal gift and the universe doesn't need your money nor your praise or critique.

And while there is a lot of stuff I love and appreciate about popular music, traditionally, in many cultures, music is not only performed by a few people with the most talent, but by all as a form of ceremony, celebration, ritual and connection. So while it might seem like you need to be a professional to play music for and with others, the more you start to allow yourself the space to play and learn, the more you'll realize that you already have the gift of music inside of you.

Music is a fundamental, universal given, gift that anyone can experience. Music isn't about being right or wrong, good or bad, it's simply the direct connection to the vibrations of life. Just like anything else, we can spend all day thinking of reasons why we shouldn't do something, thinking we must first be an expert or be in fear of judgment from critiques, yet music is far bigger than your mind lets on, you can't know music from the perspective of thinker. Step aside, let it flow through, you are born music. If you find, along this journey of discovery, that you are getting too caught up in the heady stuff, the thinker, I implore you to create a connection to music.

Put this book down, put on your favorite song, sing your heart out, dance around your room, be silly in a park, go for a run while the tunes pump into your headphones, lay down and let the music take you for a ride, whatever it may be, see what happens when you get in tune with the rhythm, allowing the mind to dissolve away even if just for a few moments.

Some of my favorite musicians to listen to that have a deep connection to music and you might find enjoyable are: Fela Kuti, Bob Marley, Talking

Heads, Phish, Ayub Ogada, Radiohead, Sigur Ros, Amy Winehouse, Aretha Franklin, Queen, and Pink Floyd, just to name a few artists that have a lot of music that is easily searchable online. You can also check out Gabrielle Roth and her 5 Rhythms Practice which is a great way to dance to a variety of different rhythms.

I also created a collection of music to help you get out of your head and into your body, all of which can be found online by a quick search of "You and the Everybody Band" or by finding me at "You Enjoy Life". Playing and dancing to music improves mood, reduces stress and anxiety and helps our entire being heal, creating a total mental, physical and emotional workout. There is an endless sea of music to help you get there, you need only to look.

When we tune in to the most simple vibration, when we

let the music move us, take us on a journey, outside of our mind, into our entire being, amazing things start to open up. As we feel and experience what it is like to be in harmonic alignment with our essence, we tune in to a knowing that exists beyond the ego. Often times it is in these moments that my biggest challenges, blocks and blind spots start to open up and shift. Other times the clarity comes after, once I have "come down" from the dance or having opened up my vocal channel, once I am calm and relaxed after releasing so much physical energy from a movement practice.

After tuning in to the music I often feel calm, collected and clear to see and feel what I was previously closed off to from the thinking mind. Your body has a perfect intelligence that often gets buried beneath the minds need to hold on to control. Surrender, release that control, and let the music take you where you need to go.

I spent ten years of my life in a band that my bandmates and I dedicated our lives to. We played hundreds of shows around the country, wrote thousands of songs, had varying levels of success and did a lot of the things that you might imagine one would do in a band. Though the experience was truly life changing and a big part of the opening up of all that I have discovered about myself, outside of the pursuit of fame and my early desires of living a life aligned with; sex, drugs, and rock and roll and what have you, over time I started to see that what I really loved about music was the pure and simple connection I felt when playing with people. As my intentions changed, the one thing that remained dear to me was experiencing music in its most basic form and opening others up to the magic that it can be in their life.

When I decided to leave my band it was a conscious choice to explore other elements of music; how music can be used as a source of healing, a medium for connection, a way to get not just a physical but an emotional workout and clearing, and a way to help people work through fear. I have since come to study a wide range of musical styles and modalities as I continue to expand and deepen my understanding of such a simple yet vast and pure energetic expression.

I love playing music with others any chance I get as well as teaching as a way to guide people to find the music within them, and tap into the power of their voice. I can't tell you how many times I've heard someone say something along the lines of, "I'd love to play guitar but I suck," or, "I wish I was a singer but I have a terrible voice," only to find that after speaking with them for a few minutes, they have these deep conditioned fears and false beliefs keeping them stuck. I've worked and taught hundreds of people with similar mindsets and one of the things that brings me the most joy in the world is helping someone bust through their fear and see them transform as they discover a wonderful musical talent laying dormant within them.

Music is a universal gift that we all share and one that we can harness, should we eradicate our fears and judgments around it all, as a way to connect to something much greater than our ego lets on. It is never too late to let music into your life, whether that be through dancing, singing in your car, picking up an instrument, or getting lost in the sound of the waves, you are music and if anyone else tells you otherwise kindly tell their fears to funk the funk off.

When we experience music, we can see the two states that are dancing with one another. On one side you have the thinking mind, the ego, the thought processor, the judger, and on the other side you have the clear channel, the energy, the vibration. There is a sort of dance happening between the two spaces and the thing of it all is to train (or trick rather) the thinking mind to unthink itself—to learn, study, process, experience and understand all that it can, just enough to drop the thinking thing when the moment strikes. I remember listening to an interview with Trey Anastasio of Phish (the band that has influenced me the most) where he spoke (though I am paraphrasing) about the value of learning the technical stuff but with the goal to condition ourselves with skills so that we can play directly from the heart.

In music you are either in the thinking mind, deciding what to play, thinking about what your fingers are doing, learning new skills, judging your performance, criticizing your voice, trying to get it right, or you are in a state where music is coming through you. Neither side is better than the other, rather they exist in harmony with one another. You can't be in both at the same time, if you are thinking about the music, you are processing it, which is valuable when you are learning new techniques, but when we play we can let it all go. When you step out of the processing part, you let it come through you naturally, without thought, for it is inside you already always, you just have to get out of the way of the fear, the need, and the concern. Explore this basic relationship and see how it shows up everywhere else in your life.

Conscious Consumption

Another energetic medium that has, and continues to have, a strong pull in my life, is food. I love growing food, shopping for food, cooking food, and of course eating it. Though I had never intended cooking to be a career, rather unexpectedly, I had a fair amount of success in the culinary world over a period of 8 years. Without getting too deep into the story, my brother and I created a popular cooking YouTube channel as well as a TV show that had us fly around the world, exploring different foods from a variety of cultures and cooking for a slew of celebrities along the way. It was a hell of a lot of fun and I am grateful for everything I experienced, but something was missing.

Like music, while there were so many things that I loved and appreciated about cooking, so much of the value of food in our culture rests on the physical and material side. Just as bands (though certainly not all) often strive to have a hit record, constructing songs to fit into a specific genre or time length, packaging it all up in a shiny box in the hopes of making it big, so much of the popularization of food was about the commodity of it, making it sellable, which has its own merits from the perspective of industry and even for the consumer, but also tends to be the thing that distracts us from what it really is about.

Over time, as my brother Mike and I started to craft a show with the simple goal of getting people excited about cooking for themselves, taking people on that journey of going from being fearful of the kitchen to showing them that they could make incredible meals quickly and even on a budget, I also started to see how much of the "food porn" element became the easiest way to sell food and thus I started to get really turned off by most of the industry.

It was a heck of a ride, and I will admit I even played into the viral nature of food myself, but as I turned away from the popularization of food and focused more on what food and cooking could really mean for someone in their life, everything started to shift. It's easy to get caught up in thinking food is really about overindulgence and eating ridiculously over the top meals when foodie celebrities from around the world are shoving it in your face, but that is only another sparkly trap that needs to be examined as we come into alignment with what does and does not serve us on this journey.

Food, like music, at its most basic level, is energy. There

is the obvious side of food when we think about ingredients, meals, and such, and ponder what we should and should not eat, but that is only scratching the surface. I appreciate having an intimate relationship with food, cooking is one of my greatest joys, cooking for myself and others, cooking as a way to create connections and build community, to improve your health, to be creative, to try new things, to be challenged, and a tool for growth and discovery. Though I don't mind overindulging from time to time and am always exploring my relationship with what I am drawn to eating, when we look at food on the most basic of levels, we experience another piece of it all.

Food is one of the most intimate things we do each and every day. What we consume becomes us. When we eat something it literally becomes a part of us. And though we often see food from the nutritional value, focusing on what we are eating is only a piece of the edible puzzle. The foods we eat, the way in which we take them in, not only in their caloric physical value, but in their energetic value, and in how we consume them i.e., what state we are in while consuming, affects us in a variety of ways. You can eat the exact same meal in two entirely different scenarios and be affected quite differently each time.

Imagine eating a burrito, in one scenario you are at work, stressed out, at your computer, shoving the food down your throat, barely chewing, as you push on with your tasks, and another where you are sitting calmly at a park, enjoying and savoring each and every bite. Each scenario involves the same dish, but can ultimately lead to an entirely different outcome because of how our body processes food depending on what state it is in.

As a creature of existence we have consciousness, which contains everything. The more conscious we are of what we consume, the more we shift our focus into alignment with who we are, and the more we evolve in a way that serves us in all that we are. This goes for food as much as it does for everything we consume; relationships, conversations, media, anything that we take in and we come into contact with, we bring it into our conscious experience, thus affecting us in one way or another.

It's a rather simple formula really; the more conscious you are of what you consume, the more you will evolve in a way that aligns with your needs. Of course it can work both ways and as we take in and consume the world around us from an unconscious state, we develop a lot of habits that don't serve us so well. But the more we bring in the awareness, or mindfulness, of what we consume, the more we see how they affect us, and in doing so naturally start to shift. Unlike dieting where we force ourselves to do something, or restrict ourselves for a short time, only to often binge and go crazy after the diet is over, when we bring in more awareness and learn to communicate with our body, we develop a natural intuition for what suits us best.

I used to love fast food, but even for years after I learned that it was bad for me I struggled to stop eating it. I would try to restrict myself, but when I finally broke the cravings got so intense I would make myself sick stuffing my face with it. But when I started to simply become more aware, slowly, over time, the more I ate it, the more I saw the direct connection it had in making me feel bad, hurting my stomach, lowering my energy, so naturally over time I stopped wanting it. Now, even the smell makes me a little queasy, and I don't miss it because I know it doesn't serve me any good.

A simple tool to bringing more mindful awareness in when you eat is to consider how you are eating. Next time you sit down for a meal, turn the tv off, put your phone down, maybe put on some light music, and take a few minutes before you eat to pause, close your eyes, check in with yourself and see how you are feeling. If you feel stressed, take some deep breaths in, do what you need to to calm down, and then start eating slowly, really chewing and savoring your food, even closing your eyes if that helps (which is one of my favorite things to do while eating).

The more you slow down and start to really savor and appreciate your food, bringing in a simple presence with each and every bite, naturally, over time, your eating habits will start to shift. As you deepen your connection to your body's intelligence by pausing and slowing down, you'll start to notice that the unfavorable food addictions you once struggled with naturally start to fade away. *Sometimes my mind is an idiot but my body and being knows all.*

The same goes for the consumption of other substances such as hallucinogens, marijuana, and other plant medicines. I've used a variety of substances, both for recreational, health and mind expanding reasons, and there is a big difference when you are doing something with an intention, doing something in a mindful state as opposed to just taking a handful of mushrooms at a party to see what might happen. No matter what we may try and do, if we look at the way in which we consume everything, we can either continue to grow our consciousness in a way that aligns with us or we can get further away from that space.

And so I bring up these things, those in which may be more of the physical, as a way to shed some light on the whole being that exists in nonduality as one. If we look at music and food as an industry thing, or a song as a clearly defined structure, or a dish for its ability to win a cooking competition, we often blind ourselves to what these things truly represent to us on a more basic and energetic level.

Our body is extremely intelligent, it knows what it needs, it can even heal almost any ailment if it is working properly, and sometimes we must only look to our mind to see why we feel the need to fuel ourselves with crap that only harms us. The more we take care of our physical body, through what we consume and how we move, the more energy we have and the more our thinking mind too is clear to see what is.

Eight
On Fear, Hate and Anger

Fear:

An unpleasant emotion caused by the belief that someone or something is dangerous, likely to cause pain, or a threat.

Hate:

Feel intense or passionate dislike for (someone).

Anger:

A strong feeling of annoyance, displeasure, or hostility.

With the way things seem to be in the world it's easy to get angry and experience intense amounts of rage and fear, even just from the thought of starting a new day. There isn't a day that goes by where the news headlines don't give us all kinds of reasons to be pissed off, upset, or worse, afraid. In light of all that we experience it's easy to feel confused and crushed about why things are the way they are. It would be easy to tell you to have hope, to be optimistic and all of that but I'm not here to say that you shouldn't get angry and upset, the last thing I would hope for as you read these words is to feel as though you can't feel what you feel, or to make yourself wrong for it. That being said, is it really worth it?

The world is a wild place, there is no question about that. All of the "rules" and "guidelines" that we live by were all, in one way or another, created by humans who, for better or worse, likely had personal gains from creating those rules and reasons as to why they made sense at the time. The world is bound by the rules we impose upon it in many ways, and in other ways, eh, not so much. It's easy to get angry when we see the people who hold the most power in the world doing the dumbest and most harmful things with it. To know that someone could be the head of an entire country and seem to care so little for people, seem to have literally no empathy and regard for those in need, can really make your blood boil.

And so I will state this again; I am not here to tell you what you should or should not feel, think, or do. But regardless of what is going on in the world right now, I still, and I mean this with complete and total certainty, have no hate for anyone living today or at any previous time in existence. How is this possible? Am I completely void of emotions? Am I so shut off from the world, living as a robotic blob of flesh only thinking in 1's and 0's? Do I myself care so little that I have put myself in a self-induced coma walled off from all human emotion and society in general? Maybe, maybe not... Truth be told, I did feel that way at first, but as I took on a new set of eyes, seeing the world as it actually was, not what fear told me it had to be, I started to feel nothing but peace, acceptance, and understanding.

You see, I used to look at other people doing bad things and my mind couldn't understand it. I couldn't for the life of me wrap my head around why someone would do something so horrible like harm another person, steal, cheat, and wage war for profit, just to name a few, when I knew in my heart there was a better way to live.

Over time I discovered something about life that completely shifted my view forever and opened up a big hole in my mind and heart that was ready to be filled with something new. It's easy to look at someone who is, say, a powerful and successful lawyer or corporation owner; they've got a big house, a beautiful partner, three kids, a pool, a brand new Mercedes, all the "stuff". It's easy to look at someone like that and assume that they are happy. To assume that their life is good, that they are mature emotionally, that they should have some grip on the world and are even possibly, company depending, a good human.

I used to be fooled by this ruse, by the facade of success, but the more I came to know about a lot of folks in these situations the more I started to see how our world was filled with grown up looking children, most of which were running the world, pretending like they had a fuggin clue. Yep, even some, okay most, of the most powerful, adult looking, successful seeming people on the planet are akin to emotional children running on pure, 100% crap fed, fear. Physically they may appear to be old, wise even, but a child they may be still. And not the fun, curious and free, wondrous and loving sort of child, rather the temper tantrum throwing, poopy pants screaming, type.

It's relatively easy to go to school, work really hard, study for your tests, apply for jobs, work your way up the ladder (even screwing over some, or many, along the way), make lots of money and get into a position of power, without ever moving an inch on the emotional maturity chart. It may seem like they are supposed to go hand in hand, that someone who is making big decisions, doing brain surgery, holding the power over nuclear weapons or leading the generation in scientific discovery, must have a grip on their emotional maturity, and in plenty of cases, some of them very well may and do. But if I had to guess I would say the large majority of humanoids simply do not, and so it is here where I want to bring up something that has profoundly changed the way I see it all, and thus the way I feel about it.

The moment I started to see just how many people, myself included for a long time, were really just stunted children on the emotional charts, the more peace that I brought into my heart. Okay now, hold up, not at first. Initially I freaking freaked the freak out! *What??? Are you trying to tell me that the head of our country, the head of most countries, might just be a child on the emotional scale? How could that be possible and if so, how could that be good news? Are you crazy?!*

Well yes, at first fear and anger flooded into my body like a sewage pipe of feces bursting in a tunnel built of hate. I was furious, scared for humanity and felt like life was hopeless. But then I started digging around a bit and discovered something that changed all of that. I started to look at where hate, fear, and anger came from. I mean really, at the heart of it, where did these feelings arise in life? Why did I have so much hate? Why did I hate things or hate people?

On the most surface level of these feelings I hated things like certain foods, movies and music. They simply didn't fit my palate. But what about people, why did I have so much hate and anger towards other people, let alone people I had never met, only heard about in the news and made assumptions based on what I heard?

When I got to the nitty gritty of it, I saw that it was because they did things that I did not like or agree with, which was mostly obvious. But no matter how bad or unjust those things were, they were still just things in the grand scale of life. Just as a cheesy pop song might not get along with my ears, the actions of certain people did not get along with my beliefs. I had all of these beliefs, things I was taught and conditioned to believe at such a young age that I held so dearly, beliefs that I was leaning on to support how I felt about certain people. But the more I dug into myself and peeled away all of my own "beliefs" to get to the truth of it all, the more I saw other people's realities as their own unique experiences. The more compassion and empathy I felt.

Someone can have horrible actions and do terrible things in your eyes, and I am not here to condone what you may consider to be intrinsically bad behavior, nor praise it or follow it. That is not what this is about. But it's like the old saying, "hate the sin, not the sinner." Being able to separate a person's actions from the person is challenging, I'm not going to lie about that, but it's the first step in letting go of your own hate and anger. Because hate, fear and anger are like a cancer growing deep inside of you.

It may be easy to point at someone else's actions and justify why you feel something, but it's a disease that grows only within you, covering your body with a grim and dark sludge of sadness and rage. I'm not here to tell you that there is anything wrong with your beliefs around right and wrong, or what is acceptable and not acceptable, only to look and see if something within your belief system might need some examining. *(Perhaps another good time to do some writing)*

When I started to look at who I had become, suddenly I was able to see why someone else had become who they had become. I stopped blaming people for their actions and started stepping into their shoes, imagining what it might be like for them. I could have gone my entire life being clueless—having my opinions, thoughts and beliefs about this and that, arguing with people that disagreed, being so sure that I was right, and being so infuriated that someone couldn't see what I saw as obvious.

But they are still my opinions and beliefs. I too, from a young age, was conditioned to believe certain things to be true, just like anyone else, but where did I get on my high horse assuming that I was right in a dualistic world? Better to focus on the destruction of my own bullshit than get caught up in someone else's.

To blame someone, no matter how old they are, no matter how "smart" or "powerful" they seem to be, for the way that they are, has become a pointless act in my life. These people had parents, teachers, or surroundings, that crafted them to be a certain way. However great or terrible they were, ultimately they were things that were out of their control. And when you look at the parents of those people, when you look at how they were raised, often times it was no different, they had pressures, beliefs, trauma, pain, and all sorts of outside influences shaping them to be who they are now.

Deep down inside, really deep down, most people are simply children, trying to prove themselves to someone, often times a parent, really just needing some love, a hug, someone to tell them that they are enough, someone to help them make sense of this wild world. And besides, hurt people hurt people, creating an endless cycle of sadness and pain.

Now I want to be very very very clear here. Just because someone does bad things and I get why, does not, in no way, mean that I agree with or support those actions, no, this is a very different conversation. You do not have to condone someone's actions to love them, or to have love and understanding for them. This is not about that at all, it's simply about reframing how you see people to get a better sense of why they do what they do and how it affects you in a not so great way. When you start to see life in this way it becomes far easier to make sense of the things that happen outside of you, the things that might seem so terrible or wrong. But it's not for nothing, it's simply the first step in breaking a vicious cycle that could drag you down a path of darkness if you aren't careful enough.

From my experience and conversations with friends, a lot of people hold hate and anger towards parents, but to realize that even your parents, the people who were supposed to be mature enough to have you and raise you, might just be scared children emotionally can really put things into a much clearer perspective. And when someone is raised in hate and fear, it's only likely that they are going to continue that pattern, and for us to be mad and angry isn't going to help the situation in the long run. We can stay stuck in our story forever, or we can step outside of ourselves, see beyond our small self, and start to shift and thus further our own growth.

So where does this all lead? What is the point? Why should I have sympathy for someone so horrible? At first I wasn't sure myself why it was all happening, why I started to change my perspective, but over time I recognized a gigantic shift in the way I experienced the world. Suddenly the superficial, outside accolades, titles that people had, and labels that were placed upon them, all vanished. Slowly, the more I realized that most people were simply scared children, the more empathy that I had for them, and the more love and understanding I had for myself. And with that, I felt a side effect that I could not have predicted; more power, confidence and hope for all of existence.

Growing up I already had hate for certain people and things. I couldn't make sense of the actions of so many, couldn't get why kids got into bloody fights in the locker room, why parents could do horrible things to their children, why countries had to go to war, why so many people were put in harm's way—the hate and fear was already inside of me, polluting my thoughts. I saw all of the things that I didn't like and often felt physically sick and paralyzed because of it. But when I realized that there was no one singular person to blame for all of this, that as humans we were stuck in some big cyclical karmic loop, parents passing down patterns to their kids, who became parents and passed down more patterns to their kids and their kids, and so on and so forth, I finally saw what had eluded me for so long.

For me, making some kind of "difference" in the world doesn't come from fighting fire with fire, or even love with hate, but from finding the core truth of it all—seeing the way things are, not from opinion, and belief, but from truth and understanding. It is from that place that I can start to make a difference, dissolve my own hate, fear and anger, and start to really see people for who they are. Not get swept up in someone else's anger and pain, but to connect to every living, passed, and future soul on this planet, to remember that we are all not so different, that deep down, we all feel pain, have been bullied, made fun of, made to believe that we are not good enough and that we don't matter. In realizing that we are all one, everyone has the universal given right to experience love and truth, no matter who they are.

We do not need to condone bad behavior, although we can stand against it if it feels right to do, but in order to really make a stand, to make a difference, we can shift our focus to lead from compassion, empathy and understanding, not from fear, for it will only consume us if we let it. If you have anger or hate in your heart, let it out, scream it at the top of your lunges, shout it out in the streets, punch the crap out of a pillow, let it be known that you are alive, that you feel what you feel, write it down, get it out. But once it's out, look at it, think about why it is really there, what good it is really doing for you, and then see if you can let it go.

Find a new perspective to live by, see people for who they are, know and appreciate them for who they are as much as who they are not, and be in that place of understanding, for that is a moment to really experience your wholeness and totality of everything. Otherwise you might just go your whole life distracting yourself with other people's shit instead of dealing with your own. If we'd all just wipe our own asses imagine where we'd be. Ever try to wipe someone else's ass? Not easy, is it? Especially when they didn't give you permission, and double especially when you don't even know who they are (warning; the writer of this has never actually tried to wipe someone else's ass and strongly suggests that you do not either, especially a stranger).

When we stop blaming the external world around us, the people and places in it, and when we start looking at who we really are and what power and responsibility we really have, that is when the needle begins to move.

I've seen people try and stand up to the "bad" people in the world, to fight fire with fire, and while I get that there are many situations where this may be very necessary and justified for those doing so, the world is shifting, and when we try and point the finger at someone and tell them they are wrong, we are likely to only make them protect and shield themselves more, hold on tighter to their own beliefs, defend against who they are, because as humans that is what we tend to do. When someone comes to fight us, even if the fight may seem just, it signals a deeply needed protection and we only fight back harder, so what good is that if we really want to make some kind of change?

I see actual children standing up to politicians and big corporations, crying on the news as they read inspiring letters about how they have stolen our planet and robbed us from our childhood. It makes me smile to think about how passionate the younger generation is and what may come of that, but why spend so much energy speaking to the people who have fucked things up so badly, and why not instead put that energy to doing right by your own terms, to inspiring others who are in alignment with you? Have you ever been in an argument with someone that you know is going nowhere? Maybe you are liberal and they are conservative, talking about abortion, or gun control, or what have you. Does the argument ever really go anywhere? Usually the person that "wins" is the one willing to push the hardest, to not give up, the one that is the most strong willed, or loudest. Sometimes people just start shouting because they get so mad and the other person simply quivers, making it seem like they've lost the argument. But does anyone ever really "win" in such an argument? Maybe so, maybe not.

I can see clearly now even if the rain isn't gone

I'm beginning to see more and more why I am writing this book. I'm not pretending that I have the answers, that would be a silly thing to think, I'm not going to act like I know the way to "fix" the world because from my point of view there is nothing to be fixed. When I step outside of myself I see things clearly, but when I step back even further, looking at the Earth from outer space, it only makes more sense. As humans, it is easy to see the world and think that things are messed up, the planet is being destroyed, the rainforests are being wiped out, global warming is coming faster than we can imagine, we have good reason to freak out. But when I look at the world from outer space, or in reality see a picture of it, suddenly it all clicks.

As humans we relate everything back to ourselves, to our own perspective, to our ego. The universe is infinite, our world is a tiny spec of sand on an infinite beach of possibilities, no more or less greater than any other. From the human perspective, from ego, things are bad, but it is because we relate them back to who we are, to what we think and believe and thus we get angry and go into fear. But as we shift our perspective to the totality of it all, which I know can be one of the hardest, if not most unimaginable things to do, and loosen our grip on what we think we know based on right and wrong, we soon realize that everything is exactly as it needs to be.

Do you really think that the Universe, or God, or whatever you call it is worried? Is afraid that all control has been lost? I've even had to consider and contemplate on a great deal of occasions what would happen if humans were extinct. Call me bleak, but I find it to be a fun exercise. The Earth isn't going anywhere anytime soon, and even if it does there is always something new being birthed in the universe. Humans might die off someday, it could be in a billion years or a hundred, but the Universe still exists in perfect harmony with itself.

Do you really think the planet, or the solar system, or the Universe can't handle a little human destruction? Heck for all we know there have been many similar planets, with similar humans on them that have birthed and dyed a million times over, maybe we are the last, the first or just in the middle, but ultimately it doesn't matter in the grand scheme because life goes on and from where I'm standing it's ALL good.

And so I am starting to see clearly why this book and I have been having a conversation, one I have been called to share with you. I'm not here to prove a point, or to convince you of anything, but rather start a dialogue with your mind. Maybe there is that part of you that wants so desperately to fit in, to be a part of something grand, a yearning in your soul to make a difference, that part of you that knows things aren't quite right but recognizes that no one has quite figured out the puzzle to this endless mystery of confusion as we spin around the universe floating in the sky sensing wonder. Whatever the thing may be that is driving you forward, imploring you to seek more, I want to remind you to keep going and that all is well.

I'm floating in the sky,
Sensing only wonder.
What has passed us, why,
Isn't it over?

I give you nothing,
And now I sleep alone.
It makes me wonder,
Will I make it on my own.

I'm floating as I die,
Sensing only wonder.
What is past us, why
Is it really over?

I give you nothing,
And now I sleep alone.
It makes me wonder,
Will I make it on my own.

-Yoshua, lyrics from the song "Wonder"

I feel extremely grateful to be living this life at this exact point in time. The appreciation I feel in this space only drives me further to share what I have seen and make it available to anyone feeling stuck who perhaps needs what I too needed at the darkest and most troubling times in my life. I in no way want to turn you off from your own pursuit of truth, justice, social betterment, or planetary saving—whatever yearning you feel in your heart, go henceforth and live it. But as I have stated over and over again, before you get to doing anything, the first step is always finding the truth of who you are and what it really looks and feels like to live in that space. Clean up your own mess, dig into the depths of your soul, and then, and only then, might you start to make sense of someone else's situation and bring forth some sort of awareness to them.

"The point is to wake up, not to earn a Ph.D. in waking up. Simply put, as Sarah surmised, waking up is job one, and then, if you still want to liberate all beings or promote world peace or save the whales, great— lucky whales — but the bottom line remains the same: You're either awake, or you're not."

- Jed Mckenna from Spiritual Enlightenment, The Damndest Thing

Nine

A Little on Judgment

J udging others, and ourselves for that matter, is one of the easiest things to do in life—almost as easy as beating our heart and breathing. Judging is programmed into us, a nearly automatic and all too often unconscious act that comes with the territory of being human. And while we may each hold different definitions for what we consider judging to be, for the sake of this short chapter, I am referring to judging as the stories and assumptions we make up about other people, places and things.

There is something so fundamentally contradictory about passing judgment that dismantles the whole idea of it the moment you become aware of it. While it is easy to assume that people are always judging you, which is a surefire way to stay small, hide your truth, and stay "inline" with the flock of sheep, in reality, you can only judge yourself. You see, people are far too busy in their own head, thinking about what they are doing, what they just did and how it went, what they are going to have to do and how it is going to go, and in general what they think about themselves and what that might mean, to really have actual space to judge anyone else (sound familiar?).

Sure, as humans we have the capacity to look at others and pass judgment—to gossip amongst friends, to go on talent shows and hold up score cards, to write reviews about a meal we just had, but in the grand scheme of things these judgments are so subjective and meaningless that they hardly need to bother even the most sensitive person.

Deep down, no matter what someone else says about you or another person, most of their mental and emotional space is reserved for judging and criticizing themselves. Outwardly it may not seem so, they may be very vocal, whether behind your back, or right to your face, but it is only, at best, their own projection, and more than likely it's their way of dealing with the fact that deep down they don't feel like they are enough.

It's funny to write a chapter about judgment and not come off like I am passing judgment on others, as though these words are somehow exempt of opinion and belief, so I will just say that the reason I know this is because I AM this. I have been there all too often in the past and even still on occasion slip into that place of "self" judgment, until I remind myself again that we are living in a sea of characters playing a role, trying to fit in and make sense of this whole life thing. Our need for judgment often stems from our desire to figure out what the hell is going on in a seemingly random and chaotic world, but it's only experienced this way when seen from the incorrect perspective.

On top of that, we are all swimming in an infinite sea of connected consciousness and getting stuck in judgment only keeps us feeling more disconnected, alone, and stuck in the illusion that we are apart from it all, when in truth we are really A PART of it all.

The next time you feel judged do some digging and write out your thoughts, examine what you know to be true until you see what is really going on. It's easy to make an assumption, to create a story around how someone else feels about you and to let it control you, but that is really just a good way to keep yourself small, to stay stuck, to keep the finger pointed outward rather than in. The attachments and ideas that you have about the "you" that you believe yourself to be can convince you of all kinds of crazy things, but the root of it is fear.

More often than not, most people are too stuck in their own head to really have any significant judgment about you that is worth obsessing about. And on top of that, the YOU that YOU think is being judged isn't even real (YOU are so much more than the human that you play), so why hold on to what someone says, or more likely what you imagine they think about that false you anyhow?

Anytime you start to feel judged remember where it comes from, get clear on where it may or may not be serving you, examine it from all sides, and see if it doesn't just fade away into nothingness. And remember, we are all connected, so whatever you think about another, is really your own projection experience to see through. Besides, don't you have far more interesting things to do?

Ten
On Depression and Anxiety

Though it seems to come as a bit of a surprise for a lot of people that I share this with, I have struggled with depression and anxiety for a large portion of my life. As a human that creates art and shares videos and writings on joy and happiness, it's easy to assume that all is good in my hood and has been for the bulk of my adult years, but you'd be sorely mistaken to do so.

Sure, I could write a whole chapter of this book talking about the experiences that I've had with friends and loved ones who were depressed, acting like I knew something about it from the outside, all while pretending I have always had a grip on it from the inside, but that is simply not the case, I've lived in a state of heaviness, sadness, aloneness and confusion for a good portion of my life.

Just like my struggles with anxiety, I didn't know that I was depressed for a large part of my life. I heard people throw around the word depressed like a sack of potatoes, "man that movie was depressing," or "that song made me feel depressed," and I could somewhat relate. But whenever I heard about someone who suffered from depression, I always thought it was something far different from what I had experienced. It wasn't until I started talking to friends, doing research, reading books, and going to therapy that I began to realize that I too had been suffering from depression and anxiety for longer than I'd like to admit.

According to the American Psychiatric Association, they define depression (major depressive disorder) as:

A common and serious medical illness that negatively affects how you feel, the way you think and how you act. Fortunately, it is also treatable. Depression causes feelings of sadness and/or a loss of interest in activities once enjoyed. It can lead to a variety of emotional and physical problems and can decrease a person's ability to function at work and at home.

And anxiety as:
A feeling of worry, nervousness, or unease, typically about an imminent event or something with an uncertain outcome.

So there you have it, the textbook, professional definition of depression and anxiety. And while I will emphasize yet again that this book is not about getting stuck on definitions, sometimes it is nice to see the box we may be stuck in so we can clearly break out of it. And rather than attempt to diagnose ourselves with something, let's look at the box, the label, and see if we can dissolve it in a way that takes care of any notion that we have anything wrong with us at all.

I can remember a number of depressive spells that I went

through; breakups, hardships with my career, struggles with my family, but early on I didn't have the awareness to really see what was happening. I saw a therapist at one point, and he diagnosed me with general anxiety disorder, but how it went down was odd and quite unsettling. I remember we had one session in which we spoke about a bunch of things in my life that I was struggling with and by the second session he was pulling out his little blue book, the DSM-5, that had all of the known diagnoses in it to see what was "wrong" with me. He started thumbing through the pages asking me questions about what I felt, reading definitions for different diagnoses, probing me to see if anything felt right. We landed on general anxiety disorder as I told him sometimes I felt anxiety in large groups, when I go out to socialize, around my partner and in some other public settings. Apparently I had anxiety and it was of the general variety. Thanks doc, so enlightening!

I was offered the opportunity to take medication to which I quickly said hell no and I am grateful he did not push me on. While I am not here to tell you what to do, I knew without question that taking prescription medication was not for me. After getting off of Adderall I never wanted to take a prescription again, and fifteen years later I still have not, not even for any sickness or illness. Instead I started searching for answers, looking for alternatives, diving deep into the cause and what I could do about it. Over time I started to become more aware of my feelings and slowly something started to open up.

Now, I am fully aware that some people reading this may be thinking about the biological or chemical side of depression and how for some medication is absolutely necessary, which I get. I am really not here to comment on that, whatever reality you live in is yours and yours alone, if consulting a doctor or psychiatrist feels right, by all means. All I am offering is a new way to look at things, an opportunity to break out of the situation you are in, to try on something different when all else has failed. In my case I realized that my anxiety and depression were situational, not some sort of chemically imbalanced plague that I was given. What I started to see was that it was more akin to something based on my view of the world, on my conditioning, and that I could grow and make the changes necessary to overcome both.

The first step in all of this was the awareness, recognizing what it felt like to be anxious, or to fall into a depressive spell and simply take note of it, not judge it, not even try to change it, just be aware of it. I was finding myself anxious around my partner, recognizing that I was creating a co-dependent relationship, that I was not able to simply hold space for her when she wanted to share her feelings, but that I took on her emotions. And thus I found myself feeling like I was walking on eggshells, doing everything in my power to not "upset" her. I just wanted her to be happy, and whenever she was upset or seemingly hurt by my actions, I made it mean I was bad, or wrong, or that I sucked, which led to me feeling depressed and anxious all while trying to avoid a "bad" situation.

I'm Not a Nice Person, I Just Play One in Real Life

I started looking back on my life and noticed the pattern that I had in other relationships. I always thought I was a sweet, kind and loving person that just wanted people to be happy. Problem was that while my intentions were pure, my actions were not. Underneath my wants and hopes was a scared little boy, a boy trying to be someone that he was not, but rather someone he read about, someone that seemed great. But my child within had not dealt with his own inner pain and so I projected my feelings on others, was not able to share how I truly felt, pretended like things were okay, and internally felt destroyed.

In 2013 I was in a really rough situation with a friend that I had fallen for. I knew it wasn't right, I knew we were not meant to be together, but I loved her, and not the good kind of love, more so I was addicted to her, something that I couldn't shake, and in turn, after we briefly got together and she ended things, I was crushed. I remember lying in bed, curled up in a ball, crippled with sadness, feeling no hope at all. I would stay in bed for days on end with no clear way of getting out, thinking that if I was ever going to be happy again that it was going to take some great universal force to get me out. Luckily it always seemed to, but the saddest part, looking back, it was all of my own design.

At the time I was surrounded by community and friends, people I loved dearly and cared about with all my heart, but with most of them I could not share what I was going through. I had painted a picture of myself as someone that had it all together, and in theory and in thought I may have, but emotionally I was a total wreck. I confused the part about self-development where you are actually supposed to develop the whole self, not just a part of the mind or the exciting parts. As I have come to find over time, my body knows best and is what holds onto trauma and pain, and that I could theorize and philosophize everything all freaking day long, and even fool people into thinking I had my stuff together, but deep down I would be crashing into a brick wall. Not fun, unless pain is your kind of kink, then what do I know?

A few years later, when Jaquy and I were living together in Brooklyn, we signed up for an advanced leadership training course. I learned a lot in that course but there was one specific thing one of my teammates shared with me that had a lasting impact, and felt like a punch to the gut, in the best way possible. One day while we were on a call she asked me how I was doing, "I'm good, how are you?" I asked in response.

"Oh no," she said. "I'm not going to fall for that one".

"What do you mean?" I said.

"I see what you are doing. You know what? You are a 'I'm good, how are you?' kind of person. You deflect your feelings, and always just want to be there for other people, which is sweet and all, but the thing is that the people that care about you want to know how you are doing, otherwise they don't know how to show up for you in your life. If people don't know how to show up for you, they can't feel a real connection, they don't know where they fit in to your life. Your friends want to help you, you just have to let them".

Damn. Boy did I get a good old whack to the face with the truth stick right there. The whole time I had thought that by being a good person for others, by showing up for them, helping them, not "burdening" them with my stuff, that I was doing the right thing, but in the end I just felt more lonely every time and wondered why no one was asking me how I was doing. Whenever I was struggling I so desperately needed someone to talk to but had a made up story about why I could not. No one was there for me because they had no reason to believe that I needed them, that I was suffering, no matter how bad it got.

That being said, I don't mean to act like I never had any support, I did have great friends who would check in on me and that I could talk to, and I am grateful for that, but so many times, when things got really dark I would just check out, shut down, stuff my face with food, get high, and sulk, waiting for it to pass so that I could put on a happy face and go back to being cheerful Josh. Even my closest of friends I found myself often hiding from. I could share small frustrations and struggles, but the really rough stuff I internalized and used bad coping mechanisms to just barely keep me afloat. A lot of the tools I was learning helped in a variety of different ways, but it wasn't actually until I heard an interview with someone that I really admire and have for most of my life when things took a big turn for the better.

A few years ago I stumbled upon an interview with Jim Carrey where he spoke about depression in a way that I had never been exposed to, it blew my mind wide open and shifted my whole perspective on the matter. I had been toying around with a similar idea, trying to get to the bottom of what depression really was, but could never quite put it into words. Jim spoke of a quote by a man named Jeff Foster and I have since managed to find the quote;

"The word "depressed" is spoken phonetically as "deep rest". We can view depression not as a mental illness, but on a deeper level, as a profound, and very misunderstood, state of deep rest, entered into when we are completely exhausted by the weight of our own false story of ourselves. It is an unconscious loss of interest in the second-hand — a longing to 'die' to the false".

- Jeff Foster

The word depressed, understood from a psychological standpoint, as per the initial definition above, makes a lot of sense professionally and medically. But if you break the word down in its simplest form, something new opens up, a key that is profound when looked at from a new perspective, when you look at it from truth.

Imagine that being depressed, perhaps from a new perspective, comes from pretending to be someone that we are not. Almost as if our body knows that when we pretend to be someone that we are not, when we hide our truth, when we shut out who we know we are inside from the world, that we get tired, heavy, sluggish and in many cases feel helpless and worthless. Instead of letting our truth shine, we pretend and create a false identity that we live in, but our body, our being, our essence knows the truth and sometimes the only way to fight it is to shut down entirely. When I am depressed I am not expressing how I really feel but instead hiding the things I don't want to share with others for fear of ridicule or looking bad. But I can't fight my truth.

And so it is in the context of the world that we live in that creates our depression and our anxiety, it's not something inherently wrong with us so much as with the false world that we are attempting to live in. Just as my struggles with attention deficit hyperactivity disorder, in the confines of "normal" society, having to sit down in class, listen to a teacher, sit still, focus and pay attention to what was going on, one could diagnose me with having something that made it hard for me to fit in to that system. But when I took myself out of the system, the diagnosis that I thought I had suddenly vanished as I realized I could do whatever I wanted so long as I was aligned with the actual world around me, not a false one created by the fears and assumptions of others.

Now, I don't want to get this confused, of course there are many forms of depression, and to lose someone you love, or go through a traumatic event may not fall into this category, not at least as easily. Feeling depressed inherently is perfectly normal and I even reckon a good thing to feel from time to time. But if you find that you are someone who is generally depressed day in and day out, or have struggled with depression throughout your life, maybe you want to look at who you have been, perhaps what false identity you have crafted for yourself as a means of survival, and what you can do about it.

That false identity may be helpful in your current paradigm, as your dream state character, but perhaps that identity needs to be reexamined, shifted, or altogether broken free from. This idea, as you've picked up on, is at the core of this book, and often times when we break free from the false, the symptoms and things we were struggling with naturally fall away because we are no longer living in a broken reality. Trying to force ourselves to fit into a world that inherently doesn't make any sense could depress even the most optimistic and happy people but this can be shifted for anyone willing to dig deep enough into their illusion.

If you are someone that suffers from depression, I'm not here to persuade you to stop taking medicine, or to avoid seeing a therapist. I've been in counseling in the past and found a lot of benefits when I found a person I could trust, for everything we do can be a bridge to the next thing. But what I'm sharing is simply something to try on, to explore as you are on this path to seeing all that has been hidden for most of your life. And besides, therapy can be freaking expensive and if finances are your fear, trying on a new concept as a first start is free, so why not give it a go? I have found that the more I broke free from the areas in my life where I was pretending, the more I started to feel a gigantic weight lifted. As the weight lifted my essence and truth naturally shined through.

Let your heart sing,
Say what you want to.
All the fear in sight,
Let today make it right

When the moment strikes,
take all the love you hide,
mess up tonight,
I wanna see you shine.
I wanna see you shine.
SHINE

Bless the daylight,
Take all that is given.
See the other side,
Let today turn out right

They may not be right,
But I am on your side.
When the moment strikes,
I'm gonna see you shine.
I wanna see you shine.
I wanna see you shine.
SHINE

-Yoshua, lyrics from "Shine"

There is something that I have taken away from therapy that has been helpful, as I have come to see that knowing something in the mind is only part of the battle. Learning to sit with my feelings and feel them has opened up my life in a lot of ways. I saw a great somatic therapist that was able to help me with a variety of bodywork as I shared a bit about in a past chapter. He is a firm believer that our body stores our trauma and that you have to work through it, not just in talk therapy, but through accessing our actual feelings.

It is easy for me to understand something conceptually, have a deep discussion with a friend about all of the things that I did in my life, what led to it, my childhood experiences, how each moment turned me into who I am and what I feel. But what was not easy was the very basic act of naming my feelings.

My therapist would start off by having a conversation with me where I would have a space to share what was going on. He would ask me how I was feeling and immediately I would launch into this whole rant about what was going on in my life, how my wife said this and the reason she said it was because of that and so on and so forth. After a few minutes he would ask me again how I was feeling, actually feeling, not the story of what I was feeling. Then he would ask me to close my eyes and check in with myself. What was I feeling in my body? What was the actual sensation?

Once I settled in I was able to check in with myself and start to actually feel, no stories, just sensations. "I am feeling a tightness in my chest, the front of my face feels warm and heavy." The more I did this, the more I named what I was feeling and the more I found myself able to process my feelings. What I had essentially been doing for many years was talking myself out of trying to feel something, an attempt to rationalize how I felt, instead of just stating the feeling. What I found helpful was the more I simply named my feeling, not attached a story to it, the more I could allow myself to feel it, process it, experience it, and either let it go, or work through it, not hide from it and only make it worse.

I share this because I want to make it clear that while a huge part of the path to spiritual growth, or whatever you want to call it, is processing your thoughts and burning that which only holds you back to the ground, to exclude the knowledge of the body from that process can be extremely counter intuitive. Tapping into the wisdom of your physical being is only going to open you up more to the truth of who you are. The mind and the body are not mutually exclusive, they are one and the same, it is only our small thinking minds that convince us, through their elusive tricks, that they are separate.

Anxiety is another interesting one. As a dear friend of mine, Eric, always says, "Being anxious never makes the situation better." Another key point to anxiety is where it comes from and the action you might take when you feel it. Let's say you are feeling anxious, often times when we feel anxiety we take an action. That action might be obsessively checking our phones as we wait to hear back from our friend that we think we may have upset, or we are anxious about our test results so we drowned ourselves in a bowl, or carton, of double chocolate fudge brownie ice cream with caramel swirls.

But the anxiety you are feeling comes from somewhere, and trying to take an action to "cure" or "fix" or more than likely "avoid" the feeling, doesn't get to the root of the problem. So what is the root of the problem? The root is fear. Ah ha, back to that elusive thing, the thing that drives so much of what we do. If you look back on a situation in your life where you felt anxious, can you see where fear led to that anxiety? I can think of a number of times in my relationships when I upset a partner, they left or shut me out, and I sat anxiously waiting for them to return, taking some action to try and distract myself from the feeling. But I wasn't getting to the root of it, I was bobbing on the surface like a rubber duck. I was afraid of what might happen to me because of my past experiences, that I was afraid to get yelled at, or hurt or lose someone I loved, and instead of dealing with the deeper truth of myself, I simply tried to avoid the feeling at all costs.

Wow, it still sort of amazes me how much of my life I spent simply trying to distract myself from feeling. But over time that has changed. When I stopped running and repressing and hiding, when I started looking and developing an awareness around my emotions, I found it easier to check in with myself. Now, whenever I feel anxious or depressed I start asking myself a series of questions:

Why am I feeling this way? What am I hiding? What am I not sharing or being truthful about? What is missing in this moment? What character am I playing, who am I pretending to be?

When I allow myself time to write and journal about this as well as sit with the feelings, not run from them, not even try to do "helpful" things like dance and meditation to try and "alleviate" them, usually things clear up pretty quickly. It is easy to want to run, but we are going to keep feeling these unpleasant things, overeating, checking out with alcohol, or whatever you do to distance yourself from the truth of who you are, is not going to help in the long run. Develop a clear relationship with your feelings, you aren't the same you that you once were, you can face the totality of you, you just have to have the courage and trust to look. When we stop attaching ourselves to what we perceive to be good and bad, or right and wrong, suddenly all of our emotions are of equal value and we can appreciate all that we feel for what it is.

And at the end of the day if the root of anxiety is fear and the root of our depression is living out a false character in a false reality that we created out of fear, whether of our own design or others, the more we break away from that world, and focus on that which is true, the more the other things start to alleviate. If you feel lost in depression, feel like nothing matters, you most certainly are not alone.

One of the times I was most depressed was when I felt like the world was all made up, full of lies, crap, and delusion, but when I started to see the bigger picture, the depression naturally started to lift. When my eyes were opened I suddenly realized there was nothing wrong with me, but that I was simply thrown into a world that can drive a person to deep depression, madness and sadness quite easily. I had a choice to stay there or to stand up, take responsibility and make a change, and as far as I was concerned, there was only one thing I had to do—get the fuck out of that false world at any cost, kicking and screaming at times, sitting and feeling at others, but I got out. And when I got out, I looked around, saw that where I had been before was nothing like where I was, smiled, and went on with my life.

Don't try and think you're someone who is broken and needs fixing, instead realize it's only your body's response to trying to fit into a societal mold that is not "fit-in-able" when seen with clear eyes. Depression is the natural response to the false world dragging you down, your body is giving you a really clear sign and instead of trying to bring in more happiness, which may work in moments, strike through the feeling, dive deeper into it, discover what it is really trying to say to you. I went into the depression instead of trying to get out of it, and on the other side I found clarity and understanding of who I really was, which was nothing really at all, which made me see ever so clearly that I was everything.

Eleven

On Money, Investments and Finances

For most of my life I would balk at hearing any conversation that had the word "investment" in it. For one thing, I didn't have any money to invest, and I always thought the word sounded way to "high profile" for me, if that makes sense. As a kid I imagined a bunch of men and women in suits and ties going into some big office building, yelling at each other, waving a bunch of money around and going berserk whenever the digital chart turned from green to red, regardless of whatever the hell I thought that meant. Of course this was some silly idea planted in my head, likely from movies, but when I graduated from college I had absolutely no interest in investing and even less so when I moved to NYC to live in "the real world".

I kept the concept of investments tucked away deep in my "screw that stuff, it sounds boring" folder, which seemed to work out somewhat okay until some years ago when I stumbled upon a book by Tony Robbins called "Unshakeable," followed by some other insightful information from others, that started to shift my perspective on money. At the time, being married, starting to make enough money to actually invest, I started to wonder if it was the "smart" thing to do. In the book, Tony and his team broke down not only the importance of investing your money to achieve financial freedom, but how the economy worked on both a physical and energetic level. Now, I'm in no way here to share all that I learned about investment, but there was one simple thing that really clicked that I think you will appreciate as it pertains to life, truth, and flow. Suddenly I went from being completely clueless about my finances to understanding money in a completely different way that helped set me financially free, though likely not in the way Tony spoke about. So before you start making assumptions, it might not be what you think.

Just to back up for a minute, when I say investment you might, as I used to, immediately think of the stock market; this big, scary, unpredictable thing that only really smart people that went to school for finance could possibly master. If so, fear not, let's take a deep breath, back up a bit and start with the basic meaning of the word.

Invest:

Expend money with the expectation of achieving a profit or material result by putting it into financial schemes, shares, or property, or by using it to develop a commercial venture.

Beyond all of the different types of investments that you can make in your life, and there are seemingly an infinite amount of choices, one simple way to look at investments is the action of giving some of your money to some sort of business, i.e; buying stock in that company in the hopes that in the long run you'll make a profit if the company's stock rises or they sell to a larger company. However, if we were to break down the word to a simple formula, one that transcended beyond the physical manifestation of money, we could start applying it to other areas in our life.

Let's say you have $100 that you want to invest in X company. If that company has stocks that you can buy valued at $10 each, which are essentially a small piece of ownership of that company, that means you could buy 10 shares of stock with your $100 (for the sake of this example we will not factor in trading fees, taxes, and other things of the sort). Now you own 10 shares of stock from X company. If, over the course of a year, for example, that company's stock goes up to $20 a share, your stock would be worth $200. If you were to sell that stock at that point, you would essentially double your money.

But investing always comes with a "risk." You could invest

into a company and lose money, the company's stock could fall, and thus your stock price would go down. Now, I could sit here and talk to you for hours about stocks and the economy, compounding and mutual funds, and all kinds of seemingly complicated sounding jargon. But this book is certainly not about that but rather truth in its most basic form. I want all of the information I share to be accessible regardless of the situation that you are in. The kind of investment I'm interested in is the one that anyone, regardless of age, skill, financial background, or other can benefit from.

And so in following my own formula for truth and understanding I will stick to just a few key elements of investing. Let's take something else that has nothing to do with companies and corporations or the exchange of money, but instead with nature. When I first moved to Denver and Jaquy and I bought a house, our house was our biggest investment we had ever made, and thus it was also the scariest.

Property is typically considered one of the best investments because you can often expect steady, positive gains over a long period of time, but shelling out your entire savings can feel like a pretty hefty risk, unlike renting an apartment. While you are fully responsible for your home and anything that may happen to it, a lot of the money that you pay towards your monthly mortgage goes towards the value of the house that you own, almost like putting money in a bank account since you can sell years down the line. There is still risk involved for sure—home values can plummet, but even so, owning property is generally seen as positive as property and home values tend to go up over time. However, there is a far more simple type of investing that I first experienced when I moved that is often overlooked but very valuable.

For quite some time I had a dream of having my own fruit trees. I am completely in love with fruits of all shapes, names, types and flavors. Right when we moved in, the first thing I did was plant four fruit trees. I went to the plant nursery, found two dwarfed apple varieties, a hale haven peach tree, a mount royal plum, watched a bunch of YouTube videos as I often do when I want to learn something new, and started digging.

As I was digging it dawned on me. Eureka! Planting a tree is one of the most simple, yet rewarding investments that you can make. I had spent most of my life thinking investing had to be this professional thing that was conducted in an office, and at least one person had to have some sort of degree in something that sounded impressive from a fancy school. But here I was, scraping at the surface of the earth, getting my hands dirty, realizing that I was making a long term investment that would reap many benefits in the future if all went to plan.

By planting my apple tree I was shelling out some money up front for something that could potentially reward me in the future tenfold. I knew it would take a number of years to get a legitimate crop of apples, and I also knew that the tree could die during the hot summer months or harsh winters, but if that tree were to survive, with a little care and love, as it grew and grew over the years, I would be gifted with a hefty apple crop for decades to come, saving me money at the market. I could also give some of those apples to neighbors and friends as a gift or trade the surplus for other fruit. Even if I moved away the fruit could continue to feed the new owners of the property for years to come.

In the process I have come to see the value of thinking towards the future. I used to be a "live in the moment" kind of guy, it sounded like it made sense and allowed me to generally stay present and relaxed, so I didn't question it. Besides, I never had enough to think too far into my future anyhow so I did the best with what I had in the moment. But then something hit me like a crisp apple to the face. *A run by fruiting!*

To think about your future is to live in your present. That may sound strange, and for most of my life hearing that would have made no sense, would have been an oxymoron of sorts, but only because I was seeing the statement from the wrong pair of spectacles. When we look at the world with blurry glasses, eventually our eyes adjust to the blur, accept it as reality, but when we get a new prescription, or even better, throw the glasses out and learn how to retrain our eyes to see properly, suddenly everything shifts into focus.

So let me say that again; to think about your future, is to live in your present. It is easy to get really caught up in this idea of "living in the moment" and trying not to stress about the future, but that is all part of the illusion of life. For starters, time is relative, not linear. All we can experience is this moment, we can think about the past, we can worry about what might come in the future, but all we have is now, whether we think we do or not. So it may seem like thinking about the future is counterproductive, which in many ways it is from the blurred perspective, especially when we stress about what may come. But when it comes to investments it makes a lot of sense. If I, in this moment, plant a fruit tree, I know I am creating something now that I will potentially get to appreciate in the future, of course, but I also get to enjoy the process now and thus don't have to worry about the future.

When I first got to Denver and planted some fruit trees all I cared about was getting them in the ground. I knew that I wanted to have fruit and figured that buying the biggest trees I could find would yield me lots of fruit as fast as possible. But slowly over time I began to enjoy the growing process, so much in fact that I enjoyed the planting, pruning, fertilizing, and caring for the plants and trees as much as I did the harvesting.

Suddenly I was investing in a future harvest while actively enjoying the present moment, a win win if I might say. I also later discovered that planting too big of a fruit tree and trying to rush the process could also hurt me in the long run, and that by being patient and getting a smaller tree, not only would be easier to care for, but would have a better chance in many cases take strong root and outgrow even the bigger trees I planted at first, which has since happened to a few of my trees.

And all my faith,
And fears are one.
And all my truth,
I tried to run.
Of all the things,
You want to know,
The things you fear,

You reap what you sow.
You reap what you sow,
You reap what you sow.
It's all that I know
You reap what you sow.

- You and The Everybody Band, lyrics from "Reap What You Sow"

And it goes even deeper. Energetically, though we may have ideas about what investing is and think about it purely in monetary terms or in the physical form, I've seen that investment can be simply about investing your time and effort into something. The word might have a specific connotation, but it shows up everywhere. If you want to build a strong bond with someone you love, whether it be a partner or a friend, the more energy and effort you invest, over time that bond has the potential to grow and grow. You can make a new friend and have an immediate bond of sorts, but the more you put in, the more you get out.

Investing in your future, while it might sound too responsible or even lame (as it once did to me) is really investing in your now. Saying in this moment "I am going to dedicate my time, money, or energy to something, in the hopes that it will grow into something big one day, while actively enjoying it in the present moment," can be pretty freaking awesome if I do say so myself. Of course there is always the potential to overthink that future and stress about it, but staying grounded and present allows you to be in alignment without getting distracted by fear.

The Most Important Thing You Can Invest In

Regardless of what you might think about investing, I would say there is one thing that you should invest in that trumps all the rest—and that is yourself.

Sure, you can read books about investments, listen to podcasts, watch people talk about the best practices, where to put your money, safe investments, risky ones, all that can be valuable and has been for me and countless others in many ways, but at the end of the day, while you can be smart and make good money playing the stock market or buying a house, investing in yourself, which really includes anything that you feel aligned with, beats any other type of investment. Now, of course there is a fine line to all of this, as putting money and energy into a home might be a piece of investing in yourself, however, making sure that our investments are in actual alignment with our true needs can be quite a different matter and worth looking at.

Funny enough I did this without even realizing it when I first moved to New York City. At the time I was fortunate to have some money in the stock market that my dad set aside from some funds I had made and acquired throughout my life (okay they were mostly from my Bar-Mitzvah). I had no idea what stocks he invested in, I just knew what they were worth, and only a month into living in the big apple, after skipping job interview after interview, I decided to cash out all my stocks and live off of about ten thousand dollars. My life focus was music and I felt like getting a job would only take away from that. I had no idea how far the money would take me, I knew my rent and utilities alone were around a thousand dollars a month, but I was prepared to go all in and was confident in this plan, however half-baked it may have seemed from the outside.

As is NYC, prices are high and life moves fast. The money didn't last me all that long but it gave me enough space to focus in those early months on doing what I loved. When I finally did have to get a day job and got hired as a private eye (I know how that sounds), I had already set up a solid foundation for my life as a musician. Having a good job, and being committed to my life as a musician felt like a great place to be. Having smelled the sweet perfume, or was it the stench of stale piss, of the underground music scene in Brooklyn, I knew what I wanted to do, and how I was going to do it, nothing was going to get in my way. And then it all came crashing down...

I'm Taking A Dive

I remember the day the recession hit. Canon Logic, the band I was in, had been a finalist in a battle of the bands competition for MTV2. We were playing the final show with 4 other bands where celebrity judges would pick the winner with the prize being an opening slot for Panic at the Disco. It was an exciting day, I was all jazzed up waiting for sound check when someone on the film crew I was sitting next to said, "Oh no, that can't be good," while pointing his phone screen at me that displayed his stock app—everything was red and curving steeply downward.

At the time I knew next to nothing about stocks so I only took note of it, shrugged and said, "Well isn't that interesting". It wouldn't be until the upcoming days unfolded that I would start to learn about the terrible recession our country was going in, and it was nosediving fast. Almost suddenly everyone I knew—friends fresh out of college, peers, everyone around me, seemed to be losing their jobs, myself included. At the time I didn't fully understand what was going on and what would come of it, but looking back it was a miracle in disguise for me.

For one, I had taken out all of my money early on, invested my time in myself to focus on doing what I loved. Even if the money didn't last long, the recession would have hit and taken a good chunk of it with it. Granted, over time the stock market goes up, as I have come to understand, the stock market and economy being like a wave, up and down, up and down. Even so it allowed me a freedom I may not have had if I was forced to get a job right away. This isn't to say that what worked for me would work for you, only that it felt like divine alignment and I have no regrets about it.

On another level, when having next to nothing, instead of panicking and getting a job, especially after my short stint with unemployment ran out, I quickly learned how to live on next to nothing. Being so singularly focused on music, instead of doing the "safe" thing, I stripped all of the unnecessary material things and extraneous purchases I used to make. I got down to the barebones, lived on my most basic of needs, and if I didn't really truly need it to survive and do what I loved, it served no place in my life. Call it minimalism, or whatever you want, I had no term for it, just a deep inner knowing to do it.

Come to think of it, the stripping away of the material items in my life wasn't that much different from a few years later when I would really start to strip away all of the immaterial, fear-based, and emotional weight in my life.

It was an adjustment for sure, but when you do what you love you really don't need all that much. The best part was that I was happy. My friends and I would get together, pool our money up, throw in whatever ingredients we had, cook meals for one another, play music, have great conversations, find free events in the city to go to, and we genuinely appreciated what we had and hardly ever felt the burden of financial strain (I can only speak for myself but I'd like to think there was some mutual thing going on).

On top of that, all of this would lay the foundation for what would become Brothers Green Eats, a cooking show all about cooking between the lines, a show for the people that didn't have a show, where we would teach you how to make epic food and live a fulfilling life without having a lot of money. I wasn't cooking budget recipes because it was the trendy thing to do, it was literally what I knew. I once spent an entire year without spending any money on food, forcing me to get creative with whatever ingredients I had laying around, foraging for free food in parks, dumpster diving, and launching my underground cooking services so I could eat whatever leftover ingredients I had. It was an intense experience but pushed me creatively in so many wonderful ways.

I also discovered something profound about the illusion behind living in NYC. Regardless of how much money people had, no matter how high profile of a job they had, how big of an apartment, or fancy of a car, practically everyone in NYC was equally broke. Now, I know that might sound absurd, it is a gross generalization, but when I started to see the truth to this something big changed in my life. What I saw all around me, no matter how much money someone had, because they were living in the city, they always wanted more. The moment someone seemed to get a promotion, make more money, and climb the corporate ladder, they felt the urge to move into a better apartment, go to fancier restaurants, buy more expensive drinks, all the while living on the edge, paycheck to paycheck, crippled in debt, just to keep up with the never ending growth that comes with living in a big city and the facade that most think they need to create.

Sure it isn't always the case, some people are "smarter" with their money than others, but it allowed me to actually feel free with the little I had. I was having so much fun, doing the things I loved that all the external material stuff didn't matter. I may have had little to nothing, but I had what I needed, so why would I ruin it by stressing about wanting more? A big part of the system we are born into is the idea that we need things to be happy, with new technology always coming out to entice us to throw out our old phone and get the next generation because of this new camera or that new screen, we are conditioned to believe that by taking luxurious vacations to exotic lands far far away will give us enough of a taste of paradise to make the rat race we live in just bearable enough, but it's all an illusion.

So where does all of this stuff bring us with investments? For one, you can invest in your own interests. Maybe there is a new skill you want to learn, an instrument you've always wanted to play, or a book you've always wanted to write (wink wink). Perhaps there is a business you want to start, and saving up money and investing in your business is a great way to build your life, but you don't even need much money to get that done, it could be as simple as starting your own YouTube channel with your phone (again, wink wink). Look around at

what you already have, what is available to you, don't assume you need much to go after your dream. It's funny, and also not funny at all, that we spend so much time looking at what we don't have, what we think we need, instead of actually utilizing the resources that are already available to us. You can make excuses all day, become an expert at knowing so much about how to do something that you convince yourself you don't have the thing that you need to do it, or you can cut through the bullshit and live your life.

Maybe you want to invest in your health, so putting money towards eating better foods may not seem like an obvious investment, but when you really think about it—by eating better quality foods, perhaps getting away from fast food and rather eating home cooked vegetables and such, as well as taking care of your health in general, whatever that may mean to you—your body is going to thrive, you'll feel better, health issues will clear up, which can lead to lower medical expenses and a big payoff in the long run. You'll have more energy, so you'll be able to focus on doing more of what you want and less on feeling like shit and complaining about how you always feel like shit. Sounds exhausting anyhow.

As you might be starting to gather, investing isn't just about buying stocks and houses, though it may be if that suits you, it's more a concept that can help you grow your life forward in all sorts of ways.

Money, or the Emotions Master

Another big key to money is that it's highly emotional, not the actual money, but our experience of it. It's one of the biggest driving forces on our planet. While many of us would rather it not be, it is at the heart of so much of what we do in the modern world we live in. Good and bad aside, money is emotional, and losing and gaining money can take your feelings on one heck of a rollercoaster ride. From my experience of living with very little, I saw that money wasn't the thing that brought happiness. In fact I experienced it first hand when I went from broke and happy to well off and unhappy. I too started to buy things because I had the money and I wanted to spend it.

I bought a house, which was fine, but then I filled the house, day after day, with more and more stuff because I could, and because I wasn't really happy. In some ways I felt that the more stuff I bought the more it would hopefully make me happy, which of course it did not. But one day I looked around and realized that I didn't need so much and had gotten into the trap myself. But as I said, money is emotional and can mess with you if you don't have a clear understanding of it.

Imagine that you made an initial investment of $10,000 in a variety of companies in the stock market. Over the last 5 years you've seen that investment grow to $17,000, a pretty significant growth, almost like free money. But then suddenly another 2008 hits and the economy drops and now that $17,000 is starting to shrink far lower than even your initial investment. Panic sets in, what are you going to do?

The more the economy dips, the more people pull out their money (PULL OUT, PULL OUT!), afraid it's all going to disappear into thin air. People stop spending as much, start being more thrifty, cutting back on what is not absolutely necessary, wondering if they will lose their job, or be stuck without being able to find one. The more fear sets in the more irrational people get, and the more stress and anxiety can consume us like a black hole of infinite sadness, not knowing how we are going to afford our home, food, all of the things that really matter, the things that felt so secure, and our life can suddenly spin into utter turmoil as we watch it all wash away.

Just like money is emotional, in a way, our economy is too. It has its ups and downs. Just as we go through different feelings in a given year, month, or a day, we have our ups and downs as well. There are times when the economy is thriving, people have jobs, money is pouring in, and there are times when things get rough. Throughout these longer periods, there are also very small micro periods where money goes up and down in small waves, but when you step back and look at the economy, it's not unlike looking at a giant wave out in the sea; the water starts at sea level, over time it slowly builds and builds up to a peak, and just when you think it can't get any bigger, it comes crashing down, a little slow at first, and then suddenly all at once, only to roll back out to sea repeating the cycle once again.

So while money is emotional and often times we thrive financially when the economy thrives, it's important to remember that the economy, just like life, comes in waves. There are ups and downs. And if you can see the down moments in a different light, you can actually take advantage of them, knowing that eventually they will go back up. In the case of the economy, this might mean hanging in there—not cashing all of your money out, but actually holding tight, knowing it will go back up, or it may mean taking advantage of the situation when it does drop.

A lot of the smart, and often rich investors consider a drop in the economy to be a massive stock sale. EVERYTHING GOES ON SALE! Suddenly giant stocks are selling for dirt cheap, half price. And that is when you can really make your money. But again, don't listen to me on actual stock advice, what the heck do I know? And how did I get here dragging you back in to monetary advice?   .

The point I am really sharing here is that the downs don't have to be bad. I got a little carried away with the financial side, but as always, it's not about that, it's about you and the journey you are on and how to stay on that journey without getting too distracted by the external stuff. It's easy to get hooked into something such as the law of attraction and see it as a way to manifest all of your desires, to put up a bunch of pictures of all the things you want; the fancy house, the high paying job, and to really do it with good intentions, but if you aren't really clear on who YOU are, what does it truly matter?

If you feel like you are having a rough year, on the down slope, hang tight, trust the process. If things are falling apart, realize that there is something else out there waiting for you just around the corner when the pendulum swings up again. Try not to get too attached to the ups and downs, they come with life, they are part of this human experience, and I have found ways to appreciate and even enjoy them both for what they are.

Sure, being in a downward spiral, whether it be financially or emotionally, sucks, there is no philosophizing a crappy feeling away when we feel it, but the more we detach from the need to be anywhere other than exactly where we are, the more we get in flow with the natural rhythm of the universe and recognize that while we are down we are most certainly heading up.

The Great Illusion

How often do you hear people saying, or maybe tell yourself, that money is tight? So often we live in scarcity of our finances, the thing that is such a big driving force in our life, but what good does that actually do? Does being afraid of not having enough somehow magically help us get more? When I was broke and living in NYC, I had very little, but I always had what I needed. I was so broke that I stopped looking at my bank account and started to simply trust that I was provided for.

It was weird at first, it freaked people out when I told them my plan, they thought I was weird or irresponsible, but at the time I was learning to trust the universe, to trust in abundance and it seemed that no matter how much I had, or what I needed, I had exactly enough to do the things that I loved and buy whatever was necessary to focus on my passions. This little process of trusting the universe and having what I needed was working pretty great, that was until I started to make money and it all got screwed up.

Once I found some success, something started to shift. I was spending more money, buying lots of "things" that I thought I needed or would make me happy, and suddenly I found myself more stressed about money than ever. I knew it was happening but I was stuck in a cycle. It wasn't until I left Brothers Green Eats after feeling stuck in it for a few years that I started to get back to a space of trust, even though I was making less money than I had.

Over the last few months, or years depending on when you read this I have adopted a similar view of money to when I was broke. It's funny to think about how and why I got off the path of trust, but in writing this book it makes sense. I had to prove it to myself by tackling it from both sides. I have more today than I did back then, but money is technically "tighter" now than it has been in a while as I navigate life through a divorce. It has challenged me in different ways, having to cut back and be more mindful about what I spend, but at the same time I am discovering something really interesting that has unlocked part of the mystery about money that I had previously forgotten about.

When we say money is tight, what do we really mean? It's easy to think about the things that we want, see how "little" we have in our bank account, and assume that we are struggling and need to find new ways to make extra money. But consider this for a second: what if money isn't tight, what if we are indeed always being provided for, always in a state of abundance, but that our finances are telling us to look deeper into the matter. What if we always have exactly enough, but we are spending excessively on things that don't matter and because of that we are pushing beyond our happy balance. Society tells us that we need more to feel good about who we are, so we buy more, and we get stuck in a violent cycle of emotional and physical debt.

Just imagine for a moment that you always have enough money and resources for the things that you need to do in this world and that perhaps the reason you are feeling stretched is because you are spending money in places that don't actually serve you. In the grand scheme of things I don't think we need all that much to live a happy and fulfilling life.

Sure having millions of dollars in the bank might be nice, or sound nice, but before we can even dream of having that much abundance, before we can really use "the law of attraction" and "positive thinking," or whatever method you've been told works to have abundance in the wealth department, perhaps we need to first appreciate and enjoy what we do have. And not by stretching ourselves so thin that we are always stressed, living beyond our means, but by appreciating what we do have and finding a way to enjoy it in the moment.

The universe is intelligent, far more intelligent than our little minds give it credit for. The mind wants so much more than it can handle and often struggles to be happy with what it has, yet the universe knows what we need and is waiting for us to catch up, to appreciate what we have, to be grateful for it, relish in it, accept it, and then, perhaps once we've started to be present and happy with what we have now, we can start to experience even more abundance. Having more money is never going to make us happier, having a better paying job or a more successful job title is never going to truly fulfill us, but if we can look around and find the joy and all around awesomeness that we are already living in, without the "need" for more, then we might just find that the more starts to come pretty quickly.

Yeah, But...

During the recent retreat I was on in Peru, on the long muddy walk out to the jungle, I trekked next to one of the participants and new friend that I had made only a few weeks before. There were a few "big" questions that she shared with me that she was struggling with after her Ayahuasca ceremonies and I told her I felt confident that by the time we made it back to the bus, which took somewhere short of an hour, she would feel much more clarity. One of the questions she had was about my perspective on always having exactly what we need.

"I get that conceptually," she said. "I may even be able to understand that in my own life if I really try, but how could you tell that to someone who is starving, living in poverty, and has next to nothing?".

It's a great question to ask, and one that I felt called to include simply because you might be wondering the same thing. How is it possible that I could confidently say that *you always have exactly what you need,* when I only know my own experience, when in fact I came from a fairly well off and comfortable family with a father that worked hard to make sure we didn't have to struggle financially? And the reality is that I can't say anything confidently, I can't even begin to convince you that I have the answer to someone else's problems, but as you may have gathered, that is not the purpose of this book. I'm not here to answer your questions, but rather get you to look at the questions yourself and free yourself of them.

Questions, questions, questions, we have so many. For every one question we assume there may be any amount of varied answers, but when you examine the question you are asking, I mean really under an illuminating microscope of detached clarity, the question begins to fade away. What I gathered from her question wasn't so much that any answer I provided was going to be satisfying to her, but that the question gave her an out, allowed her to feel comfortable in not taking action, not trying on what I had to offer about trust and always having enough.

Just because something doesn't seem applicable to someone else, just because you can find others out there, millions, if not billions of people who are deeply struggling, who, if you said, "Trust that you have enough," might laugh, or cry in your face, doesn't mean you should go on worrying about what you do or do not have. Is your worry going to make those that are poor and hungry feel any better? Is it even going to put you in a better position to be able to help those in need if that is your calling?

You aren't living in the same paradigm anymore. You aren't living in a world where there are others out there that have more or less than you do, where you should or shouldn't do something because someone else can or cannot do as well. You are not even living in a world where you know what is best for someone else, what is right and wrong, because you are one with the whole of the universe, you are connected to every living being and to act like you have the answers, or rather that you need to have the answers to solve all the world's problems, is just more psychobabble keeping you stuck exactly where you are. Destroy the questions, especially the heavy ones that only drag you down and take you away from your own growth and understanding of truth.

When you realize that the question you are asking is only keeping you stuck, keeping you in a state of assumption instead of a place of clarity and action, it becomes far easier to let the question go. If you truly do care about the wealth and health of others and want to help, why not look and see where your assumptions may be leading you in the wrong direction. If you want to distract yourself from having everything you need by asking the "big" questions that seem so important, by all means, go ahead, but why not try on a new way of being for a change, and see what happens, it's free to try, and besides, most people like free.

(While I have shared the concept of investing in the self as essentially the ultimate investment one can make, I should note; that may very well look like investing your efforts towards the destruction of that said "self" as a way to arrive at no-self. Either way, you choose your own adventure.)

Twelve

On Dealing with and Understanding Our Parents

When we are on the path to discovering who we really are there few people that tend to obstruct that path more than our parents— even if they were technically the ones that started our journey. The intricacies laid upon us merely from being birthed by people that we don't necessarily see eye to eye with are fascinating and wonderful at best, and terrifying and traumatic at worst.

As you may start to gather I did not have a picture perfect relationship with my parents. Even if you have a perfect relationship with your parents (I doubt it), from the thousands of conversations I have had with friends over the years it seems that the topic of parents, and who we have become because of them, is rarely discussed without a dive into darkness. Luckily, as always, there is truth to be had, so let's dive into it.

As a child I was rather hyper (ADHD or whatever), I would go from room to room tearing things apart, moving everyone's stuff from one place to another, before heading on to the next room like the Tasmanian devil. I wasn't a hateful or angry child, I was very loving and happy but I created destruction wherever I went and it didn't exactly make my mom happy. A lot of what I remember is from stories my parents and relatives told me, as well as videos I've watched back from the time, so in order to get to know about my childhood and relationship with my parents I had to do some real digging.

When I was born, my dad was pursuing a career in podiatry He was in residency and spent a lot of his time working and studying. Somehow, regardless of the fact that he spent most of his day working, whenever he got home he made time to play with my brother and I. I was the oldest by three years, and most of the video footage I've seen involves my brother and I climbing and hanging off my Dad as though he was a jungle gym while we giggled the night away.

Though my mom went to college and had a degree in interior design, she stopped working to take care of me when I was born, and I can only imagine how hard of a decision that was. Our relationship however, was less playful than the one I had with my dad. While I did not know this until many years later, my mom never really wanted to have kids. It's not to say that she wasn't grateful, but she got married and pregnant because it was what she thought she had to do. It wasn't necessarily a clear and inspired choice for her, rather an assumed role that she took on from the pressures of society and ultimately resented and felt dragged down by in the early years of her motherhood.

Because she wasn't as thrilled to have children as a lot of her friends seemed to be, she was met with a lot of confusion and resistance towards me, her first son. Not only was I more hyper than her friends' kids, but my mom also struggled with her self-esteem. She couldn't understand why I didn't want to be around her, sit still, or lay down with her, so she made that mean that I didn't like her, hated her even, even if I was too young to have any real concept of hate.

Of course years later, once she was able to look deep into herself and uncover her struggles, she realized that her low self-esteem all reflected back on her own struggles with her mother and her tough childhood. But at the time she wasn't in that headspace, so as the years went on I felt more and more distant from my mom.

I remember being in high school and feeling this wall between us, like a magnetic push, keeping me emotionally distant from her. No matter what she said or tried to do to get through to me, I wanted less and less to do with her. I never felt that sense of love and warmth that I heard so many of my friends express towards their mothers. Instead what I remember is how she used to get very angry and yell at me anytime I messed something up. My dad was very calm and composed most of the time, whereas with my mom little things would make her very mad and upset.

It got to the point where I would get really annoyed by most anything she did and would distance myself from her as much as I could, putting up as thick of an emotional wall as I could. She would always ask me questions about my day, about my friends, about my life, but I never wanted to share anything with her. Often when I did I would hear her gossiping to her friend on the phone about what I told her, whether it was private or not. This pissed me off and I slowly found myself trusting her less and less.

In turn, the colder I got the more she would get upset with me, expressing in frustration that I treated her like dirt, which would only infuriate me even more and I struggled to express why. It got to the point where most of her actions would get on my nerves and drive me absolutely bonkers, even being around her for longer than a few minutes would make my blood boil. This destructive relational pattern of ours went on for the better part of my life until I graduated from college and started to dive deep into my own reality and make some serious changes.

Time to Grow the Heck Up

One day, when I was in my early 20's, I was sitting on the beach with my mom and some family members as we engaged in a variety of conversations. After about twenty minutes of chatter she and I got into our usual bickering, frustrated with one another, arguing about whatever the heck people argue about, when suddenly something hit me like a shotgun blast to the face.

Maybe it was my recent delving into Buddhism, maybe it was divine timing, or maybe I just gave up on playing my usual role, but seemingly out of nowhere it dawned on me—I could spend the rest of my life acting like I was this great son, deserving of a mother who wouldn't frustrate me so much, leave me be, and treat me with the respect I felt I was owed, and she could spend her life feeling like I never treated her well and that she deserved more love and attention. Or, I could step in and make a change, recognizing that in order to clear things up between us I had to let go of my pride and see it all from the outside.

For the first time in my life I realized I had the power to change the situation, and while at first I wondered why the heck no one ever told me such obvious and potent wisdom, I eventually got over myself. I could stay in the cycle, in the loop of what I was creating, and it could be like that forever, me trying to change her, push up against her and all, as it had been with her parents and their parents and their parents generation after generation, or I could do something about it. It took me damn near twenty plus years, but when I saw the truth, I couldn't unsee it.

That night I went out with some friends and when I got home she was sitting at her desk alone. There was something about the mood in the house, it felt ominous,—but I sensed something big was about to happen. I wasn't sure what it was, I had no plan, but I knew that I had to speak up.

Upon entering the front door my mom expressed that she wanted to talk to me about something serious but that she didn't want to talk about it then. I went upstairs, but after a few minutes of my mind running into all sorts of stories I went down and pleaded that we talk then and there. She went on to tell me that she felt like I had hated her my entire life and while she could understand why when I was young, she had done so much work on herself, had changed so much, yet felt like nothing had changed between us. She again expressed that I treated her like dirt and if I would only take the time to get to know her, the new her, that things would be different.

Just as I was about to get angry, shut down and shut her out, I paused and remembered what I had discovered at the beach. I knew something had to change and getting into the same argument over and over again wasn't going to do anything. Now, I don't remember using this exact word, but according to her I went on to tell her that she had no integrity, that I could not trust her, and that all of the things that she couldn't stand about her mother were the very things I couldn't stand about her. Then I expressed that even if she felt she had made a change, the version of her that I experienced was the same person that I grew up resisting, rejecting, and maybe even hating. She started to tear up. I struck a chord.

I can hardly believe that I said what I said next, what nerve I had, but I then shared that if she wanted to get to know me, to have a real relationship with me, that she couldn't see me as her son anymore. Instead she would have to start seeing me as a person, an individual, with feelings and thoughts of his own, not just as a child who she expected things from just because she raised and birthed me into the world. As far as I am concerned just showing up and playing your part doesn't gain you assumed access to anything or anyone.

It may sound harsh, but at the time I knew I had to say it, I had to break the false bond that we had because there wasn't really much there in the first place. And in doing all of that, as extreme as it may sound, it was the first time that I finally got through to my mom. It was the first time that a real connection and conversation happened between us. This would be the first of many conversations where we would start to really dig into our past and get a grip on how things were and why they were, opening up new possibilities.

Looking back, she has told me, on my occasions that what I shared with her was the thing that really changed her life and marked the beginning of her journey of self discovery, but it didn't just end there, it trickled over to my dad too, and then other family members as I started to see the truth of what I previously thought was a never ending cycle of frustration.

I remember a conversation I had with my dad a number of years ago that previously I could have never imagined having. One day, after we had been having some personal struggles surrounding our family he called me up to chat and after a few minutes of niceties, we got right into the good stuff.

"Josh," he said. "I want to apologize for something. I feel like the reason you are struggling in your current situation is because I set a bad example for you."

"I appreciate you sharing this Dad," I said. "And you are right, I did learn these patterns from you. But the difference is I am going to do something about it."

It was in that conversation that I saw a huge shift opening up between us. He was taking responsibility and ownership of his actions and I wasn't there to blame him or get upset for the way he raised me. It wasn't going to do me any good. Rather I took responsibility for who I was and instead of wasting energy in blame, I used it to break free from my own negative patterns. It also allowed us to open up our relationship in a new way and develop a certain level of respect and love we had not had before.

Without getting into too much personal detail about my family, because everyone has their own unique experience, I started to see more and more why so many people struggle with their parents. Even though every friend of mine had their own familial story to tell, I always saw common threads. Sure, some friends seemed to have a great family dynamic, other friends were raised with one parent they felt very close to, while others were very distant and fought with their parents and ran away from home any chance they got. But there were always constants that I couldn't avoid that have become the great key to unlocking the crazy mystery of our relationship with our parents.

It's easy, and I wouldn't blame you if you resent one or both of your parents, whether they be biological parents, adopted, or other. I mean think about it; you have a mother who birthed you, literally spent nine months with you in their belly, and regardless of how equipped or excited they may or may not have been to have a child of their own, someone had to take care of you. Whoever your caretakers were, whether it be one person, or a few, they had to spend a tremendous amount of energy and effort to raise you as best as they could. To you, a child, you are born fresh, into a world of possibilities, wide eyed, ready to take it all in, like a blank script ready to be filled with stories, adventures, and wonder. But the person that raised you, whether they be a biological parent or not, had a responsibility and an attachment over you that you couldn't possibly comprehend being on the other side of the relationship.

How many times have you heard a friend say something like, "When I have kids, I'm going to do it all different from my parents," as if they know for sure in that moment that they will be a great parent, a cool parent, a fun parent, as if simply by saying it makes it so. But here is the thing, and I see this time and time again as I am at that age where friends have kids now, regardless of what you say when you are younger, when you actually have a child, all of that goes out the window.

But the question becomes why? Why can't you do things differently than your parents? Why do so many new parents live out similar patterns with their children as their parents did with them? I can't say that it's a completely simple answer, and I don't mean to generalize too much, but I want to share a basic answer to shed some light on this ever revolving pattern.

As a child, however you may be raised, it's likely that you pick up on more subtle and energetic clues than you realize. Maybe you saw your mom yell at your siblings all of the time, your dad check out by grabbing a stiff drink when the baby started crying and his partner was yelling at him, or a parent get really upset anytime they felt like they weren't being appreciated.

Regardless of what you proclaim you will do as a parent, when you actually get into that situation it is likely that when things get tough you will act based on what you know and what you have seen growing up. A lot of new parents repeat similar patterns to their parents because once emotions take over, when they are stressed out, knee deep in diapers and shit, struggling to remain calm , when their Zen practices go right out the fuggin window, suddenly the patterns they picked up from their parents come out and in many cases take control of the situation.

I'm not saying by any means that this is the truth across the board. I've seen great parents really commit to raising their children in a way that is far more conducive to parenting than they were raised, but it does happen quite often. Suddenly you are thrust into a role that you don't have any experience in and you do what you know, which is likely what you saw was done when you were growing up.

And it is with that that we can begin to see the key to understanding our parents. You see, our parents are on a loop, just as we are, repeating history with slight variations over and over again. They are conditioned beings, as we are, that take in the world around them, good, bad, trauma, love, pain and all and exist, often blindly from this place until perhaps one day something shifts and wakes them up to the truth.

But that isn't reason to blame our parents, because the truth is, if we look back at their parents and their parents' parents, and so on, we can trace these patterns back for generations. Sure, culture changes, things change, but these habits go back further than we can hold blame for. I could hold my parents to blame, like I used to, becoming upset and angry

—why did they do this to me, why couldn't they just be how I wanted them to be, why did they have to make things so complicated? As I smartened up over the years of seeing them for who they were, suddenly it all made sense. Regardless of how sure I was that they were a parent to me, or that they knew more than I did, they were still just kids inside, kids who had kids, who had to then step into the role of parent, whether they were ready for it or not.

And yes, I could say it is their responsibility to step up, and plenty of parents do in many different ways, but I don't need to hold hate or blame when I see clearly what life is. Who am I to say that they should or should not have done this or that? What good is that going to do? Just more judgment, more stories, and more assumptions that I know something more than them without actually living it.

Maybe your relationship with your parent has to change, maybe it isn't going to be what you thought it was going to be, maybe you won't even talk to your parents for years, or maybe suddenly you become close to them when you never thought it was possible, but regardless of what happens, holding onto blame for your parents is just another way to stay small, to hide yourself in a locked cage, and always have an excuse for why your life isn't working out. Break out of that box, find a way to forgive your parents, to let go of that frustration, that hate in your heart. Tell them you love them, or why you've hated them, and find a way to extinguish the blame, not by faking it, but really feeling it, and go on to parent your own life. It's time for you to take matters into your own hands. Perhaps you've pointed the finger outside of yourself long enough.

I have nothing but love for my parents, I am truly grateful for all they have taught me, all they have provided for me, and all the love I have gotten from them. I no longer compare them to other parents, wish things were different, I don't know where my relationship with my parents will ultimately lead, but I know I have nothing but love and respect for them, as human beings, not as imaginary superheroes that were supposed to save me but kept failing to do so.

Parents are people, they did their best, no matter how good or bad their actions were in your eyes. We don't have to put up with bad behavior of parents, or condone terrible things that have been done to us, but making assumptions about what we deserve doesn't get us anywhere. Let go, look at what you love about yourself, appreciate that, and sure, you'll see what you don't like about yourself, but find a way to guide yourself out of this cycle, create something new, try something different. Haven't you stayed in the same story for long enough? Are you not bored? Are you not ready to watch another movie? I know I was.

The Changing Is The Hardest Part

The last thing I want to express in this chapter is about the whole "if you want to have a relationship with me you can no longer see me as your son," thing I told my mom. As an individual it is natural for us to want to break free. While we were born into this world with our own identity, our parents had years of being responsible for us where they may have merged their identity with ours far more than we have with theirs. It may be the reason why we want to get away so badly and they want to keep us so close. We are experiencing opposite energies in many cases, but at the end of the day, it all goes back to ego and fear.

Yes, biologically we are our parent's children, but that doesn't mean we have any specific obligations because of that. On the path to waking up, everything must be examined, and in some cases, mostly everything must go. Dissolving the false self and dropping the ego is a full experience, we can't half drop the ego or partially destroy the self. I mean you can try, and you might have some luck at exchanging your bad habits for better ones, that's fine and all, but if you really want to wake up, you must be willing to risk it all; family, friends, career, food, movie preferences, all of it

This isn't to say that these things have to go for good. I didn't speak to my parents for nearly 2 years at a time when I felt like they were only hindering my process of aligning with truth. I made a choice to separate myself from them, however hard it was, because I knew that I had to, and knew that I could. Things are good with us now, I let go of the character I was playing, tore up the story I was telling myself, and dropped the idea that because they raised me they ought to treat me a certain way. I no longer see them as parents in the way that I used to, now they are simply people that I appreciate, enjoying talking to, and do so because I choose to, as they do with me, not because I am supposed to for this reason or that.

It wasn't easy to make these changes, as I can imagine it wasn't easy for them either, but I knew it was necessary, and it was something I even questioned, however weird it felt at times. In order for me to discover who I really was, I had to be willing to lose all of who I was, and when I did, when I burnt my house down, then, and only then, did I release my attachment to the stories that were keeping me captive, and actually grew up and find out who I actually was. So while the act of examine everything in your life may seem scary as all hell (and it certainly can feel that way at times), it's not because everything must go, but rather in the search and willingness to look that we get to see what serves us not.

Thirteen

The Unwinder

As I go forth in this life, taking in its sweet smells,
Gazing at its divine sights,
harrowing in its lies, Intoxicated by its lives,
I am consumed by it all and I remember once more,
All is exactly as it's meant to be.

Overtaken by its magic and fantastical wonders,
swept away into its silence, destroyed by its beauty.
I close my eyes to remember what it all feels like,
away from the distractions,
from the toils of trouble,
and I am free then and now.

Amongst all that we have,
divided and undivided, all is here.
We may travel into these places of glory,
yet we take on their eternal stench.

Unwind the moment,
see it all, through the veil,
beyond the untruth,
feel the remembrance of all life's golden moments,
brought together in all points in time.

When you have found the answer to this,
when you have seen this for yourself,
then, and only then shall you know all that there is to know,
which of course, is nothing.

Somewhere amongst these conversations,
somewhere along the way, the truth to all has been revealed.
Life's greatest mystery is no more.

As a brief reminder—words and language, however wonderful and powerful they may be, can also be, in many ways, a really poor way to communicate this stuff, strange as that may sound. I do what I can to write to you in a way that makes some sense, and I trust that it does, but I want to remind you not to get too caught up in the words. The words of our conditioned language can only do so much to explain that which is hardly explainable in such a way. I like to invent words from time to time because I recognize that our current language can only explain that which it knows, and thus it can feel limiting to explain something that is unexplainable in the current paradigm of how we communicate.

If what I'm sharing makes sense to you then forget I said anything and keep going forward. But if you are getting tripped up, try and only remember that words are like a blurry map that can be of some assistance in helping us break out of our false narrative, but can also keep us captive if we give them too much credit.

Fourteen

A Conversation With
My Best Friend About Self-Doubt

A lex is one of my oldest friends, not by age (we are about a month apart in actual age), but I have known her for about 20 years and while our friendship has come in waves of connectedness, no matter how long we do or do not talk, our bond always remains intact, only strengthening with time. Looking back at our friendship is always a reminder to me of how far we have come, from silly teenagers at a time when I refused to have serious conversations ever (something that Alex reminded me of not that long ago), to the beginning of our journey within, and even now as we are taking life as it flows into us.

I wanted to include a recent text conversation we had to attempt to demonstrate what typical conversations are like with some of the people that I am closest with in life. I didn't always have these types of conversations, and while the inner journey to truth is shrouded with a lot of mystery, intense work, and hardship, it can also be a lot of fun and you can make it light and as silly as the moment requires. I could publish a plethora of conversations between us over the years, ranging from the more than slightly absurd, to the extremely serious, as we've been a huge support system to one another through all sorts of life's wild and wonderful phases. Always being that reflective mirror reminding one another to go forward, that we are not in fact crazy, and that everything is as it should be.

In the following conversation that I am sharing about self-doubt, it might seem that early on I am taking on the role of teacher and helping her work through something, but I know better than that. I'm not here to "help" anyone any more than they are here to help me. It's a give and take of sorts. As I share my perspective on something she is struggling with, I am working out how to better express it myself, and in doing so, share it with you. Alex knows the drill and I know that as soon as she starts to get some clarity in the conversation that our roles will shift and she can be just as much of a guiding force for me to break down whatever invisible wall is in my way.

I used to get in to all sorts of relationship and friendship dynamics that were very one sided, especially when I first started on this journey, I just wanted to help everyone I could, shake people awake, unsolicited advice and all of that, but I quickly felt isolated from the world and in the long run it did me no good. When it comes to friends I'm out to create dynamics that are mutual, to have allies, to have friends that don't idolize me, or I them. I'm not here to amass followers or believers. The same thing goes for you, yeah I'm talking to you, cut my (metaphorical) head off already dammit!

The following excerpt is from a text conversation we had while I was in Peru and she was back in Maryland right after she got offered an exciting new job.

Alex: "I'm noticing how hard it is for me to allow myself to celebrate my accomplishments. This feels like a big step in my work and I go straight to fear"

Me: "FUGGIN CELEBRATE THAT SHIZ! Or don't, it will all still end up fine." :)

Alex: "Haha I'm working on it. Mostly just observing myself and my egos reducíos esa."

Alex: "Ridiculousness*"

Me: "I prefer reducíos esa."

Alex: "But it feels so real sometimes. Haha that was good." (referring to the accidental auto correct)

Me: "What feels real?"

Me: "Like a Harry Potter spell" (referring to the autocorrect)

Alex: "My intuition."

Me: "What do you mean?"

Alex: "Oh, that this job is a good thing and I need to just receive it and chill out."

Me: "Ah yes. But there is a part that you are fighting? Like fighting intuition?"

Alex: "But self-doubt says, this is super important and you're probably not good enough for it."

Me: "And going to the negative. Ah..."

Alex: "Yes This is a pattern."

Me: "You know the funny thing about self-doubt?"

Alex: "What?"

Me: "It's funny because in reality there is no self so how can you doubt something that doesn't really exist? :)"

Alex: "I get that on like a conceptual level, but not so much on an experiential level."

Me: "As I've been putting the finishing touches on my book I re-read the first Jed book the last few days and have had some big slap in the face reminders."

Alex: "Yeah? Like what?"

Me: "Well, like a lot of normal human problems don't get solved by solving them, like stress, anxiety or depression, it's not in the trying to cure them that gets cured, more like when we see the truth of who we are, the side effect is that they naturally start to fade. And I suspect self-doubt is the same. The only real way to conquer it is to abolish the very idea that you have a singular self that needs to be doubted."

Alex: "Yes! That I totally get, especially recently."

Me: "Not by trying to be less doubtful or something ya?"

Alex: "For me, the way to abolish that is to connect more deeply with my higher self. And the more I merge with my higher self, soul, god, whatever, the more those seemingly real problems of anxiety and depression, or lack or dissatisfaction or stress disappear. AND the more my external world begins to look and show up very differently, and this job is a great example of that. So maybe that's a different way of framing the same thing."

Me: "I hear ya. Yeah. I would define 'higher self' as no-self."

Alex: "Or oneness?"

Me: "Because in order to experience what we are sort of defining as 'higher self' we need to blast through the illusion of this small self. Same thing yes oneness."

Alex: "Oneness is another thing I get conceptually but not so much experiential."

Me: "How so?"

Alex: "And would you also use the word source or god to describe the no-self?"

Me: " ps. Words aren't the best way to describe things, so much can get lost in translation if you know what I mean."

Alex: "Yes this is true. Especially when describing something so esoteric."

Me: "Sure you can use god. God mind, oneness, non-duality. No-self. Truth. All just words we made up to describe something far beyond words. So anything we define as self, when we start slashing at it, examining it, digging, we see its' built only on lies, on made up concepts, as a way to define ourselves, to hold up our ego."

Alex: "Yes I see."

Me: "We try to make sense of the world through belief. Instead of just burning it right to the ground."

Alex: "I get that."

Me: "And basking in what is left."

Alex: "Haha."

Me: "haha. Burn the fucker down!"

Alex: "This job is a great opportunity for that, because the fear is about it not working out or me fuggin it up. But while noticing these things come up, I also totally trust whatever happens as perfect and my job is simply to be present."

Me: "#truth. Something that I've been playing around with a lot today that also shifted things, and I posted about sort of on Instagram is that when we have a question, it's not in the answer that we get clarity, it's in breaking down the question. I think fear works the same way. I'm noticing how easy it is to think something such as "my fear of going into the jungle is that I'll get sick and won't have a good time. But as I examine the statement I realize it doesn't really hold any weight. So what if I get sick, or don't have a good time, what does that matter in the grand scheme? Ya know?"

Alex: "Yes exactly! And when I break mine down I'm like "so what if it doesn't work out or it all falls apart with the job? Like literally doesn't matter. So while I have the experience of fear, I also know at the same time that it's 100% not real . And this conversation is helping me get that."

Me: " :) I'm just a reflection of you/ The only person we can't directly see is ourselves so we can be reflected back from the people in our life. Helps me too."

Alex: "Indeed. Thanks for being such a great one!"
Me: "I think our conversations could have easily just been a part of this book haha."

Alex: "How are you? I was gonna message you earlier but thought you were already in the jungle."

At this point I went into sharing some struggles that I was working through, I am not going to include this part of the conversation simply because I have shared enough about myself and my struggles, which in this case involved romance, relationships and the side of me that craves and needs others' validation. But I'll spare you that stuff for now.

It is easy as you go through this path to acquire a lot of knowledge, whether it be self or external knowledge, and to conceptually understand things but still get frustrated when your emotions seem to struggle to catch up. But that is the beauty of having people in your life that you can talk to, that get you, that can be that truth mirror of self-reflection, reminding you that whatever you are feeling is okay, guiding you to flow through it.

Even when you wake up to truth and dissolve the ego, you still have to exist as something to converse with people and the world, so slipping back into the ego state is a natural thing to do. And even if you are no longer attached to it, sometimes it tries to rope you back in, trick you into thinking you have a small self that needs "things," but it never lasts for too long and having a good friend as a reminder, or a mentor, or a book can be all it takes to get you back in line with your natural flow.

Sometimes I find it is best to just listen, sit back, empathize, support, and oftentimes that is all it takes to be a good friend, you don't need to have the answers, just to listen attentively and support. Other times it's fun to test out different ways of expression and sharing an idea that might open the person up to something new, and other times even the conversation calls for some blunt truth bombs to the face. It's good to get a sense of what the conversation requires, whether that be listening or helping to guide, with close friends you learn over time.

In the case of Alex and I, we both know that whatever the person is saying is only coming from a place of guidance, support, deep respect, trust and love. When she reflected back to me the things I was struggling with in relation to my neediness, I knew it was because she knows me well enough to help me continue to spin my wheel. Once I start cranking the lever, it's all about momentum, and keeping it going so the wheel gets faster and faster. When the wheel is starting to get to full speed, all I can do is continue to turn it until it's spinning fast enough by itself, and eventually it runs its course, slows down, and gets to the place it needs to go.

Sometimes it is the momentum of a conversation that allows us to break through it. The thing we are dealing with in the moment might seem small, silly, even petty at times, but instead of denying it, instead of pretending that I am some perfectly formed human that doesn't struggle with "little things" like social media addiction, relationships, and attachment, I go deep into whatever feelings are coming up, and the more I express and share them, the more I dissect and unwind the very nature on which they were built. And in doing so, the easier I find it is to let them go and shift my attention to what is and away from what is not.

I used to think being awake, or enlightened, or whatever other silly word one might use, meant that all of my problems, worries, fears, and negative feelings would go away. But if you were to drop me in the middle of the ocean surrounded by great white sharks, you can imagine I might piss myself silly. Once you see life for what it is, in one sense the work, the seeking, the journey might be over, but in another it has just begun.

When you shift from one reality that no longer makes sense, to another that makes perfect sense, life doesn't suddenly become some blissed out, at one with God all of the time, state, as you may have imagined it to be, or even a boring one with nothing to do, nothing to feel, nothing to experience. The shift is really quite simple actually and it's hard to explain until you've gotten there yourself, and when you do, you may not even have an interest to explain it, should you even realize what it is. I wrote this book because it felt like the next thing I was supposed to do, but you may choose to move to the mounts, be a hermit, and live off the land or continue on with your job as a doctor and not change a single thing. Waking up doesn't look like you probably imagined it to, which may be the very reason you've struggled to accept what has already shifted in you. And if that is the case, that is perfectly fine, because all, as I will remind you, is exactly as it is, no matter what you do or do not do.

Fifteen

On Friendships, Relationships and Non-attachment

At different stages throughout my life I've had quite a diverse grouping of friends that continues to change with each passing year. Some of my oldest friends are still some of my closest, others continue to flow in and out of my life as I make new friends in each new place I go, and while I am extremely grateful for the bonds I've created over the years, there was one thing I never fully understood.

In elementary school I was a nerd, I spent every second of free time with my nerd friends (even if we didn't consider ourselves nerds)—we played video games, had sleepovers, collected bugs, played roller hockey in the street and road bikes throughout our neighborhood. In school I was bullied by the "bad kids," picked on for being a dork and made fun of. In Middle School I was befriended by one of the schools notorious trouble makers, sent to detention, smoked my first cigarette and always seemed to be at the heart of trouble just before being swept up by the cool kids for reasons beyond my understanding.

I suppose you could say I enjoyed this new grouping of friends, but truth be told I never really knew why they wanted me around and in the back of my mind wondered when it would all come crashing down. In High School I felt my life split down the middle—on the one hand, being a football player, I sat at the table with the other jocks as they made jokes, talked about girls, sex and partying and teased and played pranks one another, seeing who could be the most outrageous and garner the most attention. On the other hand I was on medication for my A.D.H.D and mostly sat with them silently giving away my lunch in favor of studying for tests and finishing up tomorrow's homework. When the medication wore off at the end of the day and after school my friends appreciated me for my sense of humor, we had a lot of fun together, and I enjoyed going to parties. At the same time I was dating a girl that went to a prep school and though spent a lot of time with her, she ran with quite a different crowd, I never felt like I fit in or was embraced by her friends, and thus felt uncomfortable and out of place most of the time.

In college I started a band with my roommate—we spent almost every waking hour playing and writing music, only going to parties and hanging out with other friends when we persuaded them to come over or on the rare occasion that they persuaded us to leave our music cave. I made a few close friends that I really cherished, including my bandmates, we had a lot of fun in our own little world, mostly uninterested in what was going on around the college campus, I was so hyper focused on music that nothing else really seemed to matter.

In Brooklyn, finally feeling a great sense of freedom, I turned my living situation into a sort of communal space with an open door policy. I started persuading my friends to move into the same apartment building, filled with artist lofts, befriended all of my neighbors, was called the "mayor" of the building, became the guy that threw parties that everyone wanted to be at and had a heck of a time, even if it did get a little out of hand and in some ways I felt like I got walked all over for not setting up any boundaries or guidelines to our space. When I met Jaquy we moved in together and focused on creating a home, a place where we would have a sacred space, one with more guidelines as we crafted the life we thought worked best for us.

When I moved to Colorado, having learned from so many years of building friendships, I started to do things differently, focusing on what felt right, building community that didn't necessarily have to be in my own home, and befriending people that I felt aligned with, that I cherished spending time with, not doing things out of wanting to be liked or needed (as I eventually saw I had in the past), and focused my energy where it flowed most naturally. I've had a wide range of friendships in my life, all that I have cherished in one way or another yet when I look back, I can't help but notice specific patterns.

On the one hand I would start out in a place, such as college, desperately trying to make as many friends as possible, being the social guy, going from room to room, dressed in some silly outfit, to meet all of my neighbors. I would have half of the freaking kids from the dormitory in my phone number, getting invited to a bunch of different parties, and constantly be pulled in different directions. Yet as my interests came into focus over time I would drop the search of numbers and in my last days be surrounded by only a few friends that I cherished deeply.

The same thing happened in Brooklyn, going from epic party throwing guy that new everyone to intimate group of dear friends that I loved and trusted. Having a small grouping of close friends that I feel aligned with has been invaluable, and though some of them have remained constant throughout my life I started to notice something interesting about how friends came in and out of my life.

One day I was hanging out with a dear friend in Brooklyn, a fellow musician, one of the most talented singers and songwriters I've ever met, that lived not a block away from my building. We were deeply engaged in a talk about some of our favorite musicians—what made them unique and special, how they created music from such a tuned in and purely vulnerable state that moved so many of us, to this day on such a deep level, when something hit me. My friend, in this moment, reminded me of another dear friend that was a big musical influence to me in the past, someone that I had lost touch with over the years. Not only that but when I really thought about it, they both had a similar energy of sorts, even looked similar and had oddly close facial features.

It began to feel like I would lose touch with one friend and create a new bond with another and in looking at the friendship see certain similarities almost as if the energy of my friend, say Charles, the trouble maker, that I clearly attracted in Middle School, would show up in a more evolved, a more conscious and aligned version in a new friendship. As if in letting the now broken tie go of one friend would make space for another to come in that would only harbor my own growth. It made shifting friends a lot easier, not tirelessly trying to put energy into old friendships that weren't working anymore just for the sake of keeping something dead nearly alive, but to see the shift and growth that comes when we let go and allow new energies that match our frequency to come in.

I started experiencing friendships in a new way, I saw the friendships that lasted in my life, those that remained constant, and how those friendships found a way to continually evolve as both of us grew and changed, and I allowed the ones that weren't working to naturally fade away. It's not like I've had to "breakup" with too many friends, it was usually the case that the universe took care of it in all of it's mysterious ways, whether a friend and I moved away and lost touch, or things naturally faded, I always found that new friends would come in to expand on what the previous friendship had once been for me. It made making, and losing, friends a lot easier, I wasn't so attached to forcing things to work that were not working, and allowed energy to flow gracefully, but when I started to dive deeper into non-attachment, I found that making friends became a struggle for a reason I had not expected.

There is a common misconception when on the "spiritual path," or when searching to attain "enlightenment," or whatever you want to call it, that all of your attachments; friends, family and the like, must ultimately go. This is one of the many things that keep people stuck, the very idea of letting go of everything and everyone that you love is enough reason to quickly run like hell as far away from this place as possible. But as I've come to see, it's not like that at all.

In the context of the "normal" world, or of living in our ego, yes, we have to dissolve the false and that means letting go of a lot of the good, the positive and the things that we think we love as much as it does letting go of the bad, the harmful and the negative. To really take a look at our life and discover what has led us from ego, from the past, from falsehood, from fear, we soon come to see that most of what we think we enjoy—the friends that we think that we always wanted, the job we thought we needed, and the things that we thought would make us happy— all have to be examined and ultimately let go of in order to take the next big step and move forward on our path. And while letting go of not just the bad, but the seemingly good sounds scary, that doesn't mean we can't attach ourselves to things, that we can't form meaningful friendships.

In the process of waking up, of living in a state of non-dualism, of seeing everything for what it truly is and is not, while it becomes abundantly clear that the world we have been inhabiting only exists on meaning created from falsehood, that doesn't mean we have to let everything go, sell our possessions, become a hermit in a cave, a monk or a recluse that renounces all material objects. It might seem like that is the obvious path to take, and for some it very well may be, but it may also be the thing that keeps you stuck, because it feels way too scary to let go of and much easier to stop your searching and settle down into comfort. In order to best express this point I want to talk about non-attachment a bit more and the misconceptions that often come with it.

When I first learned about non-attachment from Buddhism it made sense enough. If we attach ourselves to things that are always changing, then, once they have shifted, we experience suffering because life is impermanent. It took some getting used to but seemed simple enough— don't attach yourself to anything unless you want to experience suffering. That quickly led me to a path of emotionally distancing myself from anyone in my life and instead attempting to form connections based on the student/teacher role and not on feelings or to create equal bonds.

It worked well enough at first—I started distancing myself from friends, only keeping relationships around me as a way to help others grow and learn, and whenever I would meet someone new instead of being vulnerable and honest as a way to create connection, I took on a sort of "I know all and I can help you," persona and kept my distance. I wasn't consciously doing this in any sort of deceitful way, I genuinely thought that to be in non-attachment there was no other way to interact with people.

And though I suppose it had its merits, I eventually became very lonely and stuck. Over time I brought my walls down and started to let people back in, which was fine for a while, but I slowly saw that I had yet to deal with my own issues of attachment and neediness and thus created new friendships and relationships based on fear and a need to be loved which only exasperated the cycle again. I thought that non-attachment actually meant having no attachments, which seems like it obviously does, but then I discovered something that allowed me to dissolve the illusion of this dance once and for all.

To see non-attachment as a good thing, and attachment as a bad thing, to always be wondering if, in order to grow on your spiritual path, you must make sure you are living in one state and not the other, often only keeps you stuck, keeps you in a loop where you are constantly questioning whether you are doing it right or not. It's like wondering all the time whether you are being "spiritual" enough, comparing yourself to other "spiritual" people, buying more crystals to make sure you have enough positive energy flow, being sure to go to Yoga and post about it on your instagram so everyone can see just how woke and aligned you are.

Having a spiritual practice, seeing energy healers, being a psychic, within the context of consciousness can all be as real and powerful as you need them to be, and if they work for you, great, I know a lot of talented people in a variety of these fields, some which I have found very helpful, but if you assume that any one thing or person is going to "fix" your life for you, you may be in for a rude awakening. It's all part of the illusion, of Maya, of the false-world designed to keep us stuck. It is in the false perspective of attachment and non-attachment that we stay in suffering, in clinging, regardless of which one we try and be in.

Now, with the illusion dissolved, I no longer wonder whether I am being attached or not attached, I don't avoid making friends, getting into relationships, or trying and buying new things out of the fear that I might fall into a state of attachment, because attachment isn't a physical thing, it's not even an emotional thing—it's a false thing, a made up idea thing, one that needs only to be dissolved in our minds.

Now, I create whatever friendships I want to, I fall in love with people, I dive in head first. I'm not worried about whether things will shift or change, I'm not questioning whether they are wrong or right, or if they will lead me in a good or bad direction, I know and trust that what I am attracting is exactly what I need. I can experience friends and relationships as they are in the moment, and should they shift or change, I can shift and flow with them. It's not to say that you shouldn't make decisions that feel right, but only that the more you tune in to who you really are, the more those decisions become obvious.

Contrary to popular belief about the awakening

process I even get sad, I experience my own insecurities and neediness, I feel my heart break, and instead of judging myself, or getting down on the fact that I have these supposed "negative" qualities, or should be in some other state, I simply look at them, become aware of them, sit with the feelings, and allow them to be until they are no more. It might seem like the path requires us to always be in some elevated blissful, happy perfect mood, but we exist in whatever way we exist in this very moment. We have feelings, thoughts, beliefs, ideas, emotions, and so what? Once you've dissolved the false, seen through what is not true, and experience life beyond the dream, beyond the false self, you can drop the whole wondering and worrying thing and trust that what you are experiencing is exactly as it should be.

The awakening process is as it is, dissolving of the false self, of the ego, experiencing no-self doesn't come with the same cost as we assume it to. We still have choices, we can still pick up our old character in some regard, or create a new one as a way to interact with the world, to enjoy the company of others and converse about our hearts desires, to communicate with the man at the checkout counter, but we no longer get caught up in it all. We still have preferences, we have likes and dislikes, we have opinions, dreams and hopes, things we want to work on and grow, but our relationship to these things shifts. And so when we create friendships and bonds in the new space we no longer create them out of the false, not because we try so hard to be authentic, but because we simply are, and whatever is is.

I CAN stress this enough, I really can—the trap, the trick, one of the final illusions is comparison. When we keep holding on to what we think things have to be in order to attain some sense of "oneness" from the state of the ego we only keep ourselves stuck in a mental prison. It might seem better on this side of the bars, with all the wardens and their weapons, but we are still in jail.

So I say make as many friends as you want, buy all the things that your heart desires, fall in love, have your heart broken, run outside screaming at the top of your lungs how ridiculous life is, whatever it might be—when you are being guided by something much greater than the false material world, when you've truly looked at who you are and discover your infinite nothingness, when you've dissolved the ego, then whatever is simply is and you no longer have to wonder whether you are getting it right, you know that each and every breath you take, every inch of you, it's all as it is meant to be and you can experience it HOLY.

When it comes to the actual side of making friends I

will share two final points. First off, follow what feels right. You may know a lot of people, but to really get to know someone, to connect with someone that gets you, that you feel comfortable enough being yourself around can in many ways be priceless. Sure it's easy to say that you should be comfortable around yourself no matter what, and in time I trust that will be the case for you should that feel called, but it does take a certain level of dedication and time to create a friendship and I'd rather have one real friend than 3000 people on facebook that are labelled friends that I hardly know. Don't focus on the quantity of the friendships you want to have, it all goes back to quality and connection. And the trick is, there is no separation between you and others, so the friends that you have are just as much you as you are them.

Thinking you are separate only plays deeper into the false idea that we are individuals, that there are others "outside" of us, we are all one in the endless dance of this thing we call life. Making a friendship, one that feels authentic, is really just another part of yourself that you are getting to know on a deeper level as you discover more of who you really are. And connections come in many forms—it may be with a "real" person, which seems obvious, but a friend may come in the form of a book (hint hint), a distant relative that you find yourself drawn to, even plants and animals. Whatever sparks your curiosity, whatever lights that fire or makes you feel more at home, or at one, or simply draws you in naturally, may be something worth exploring. When you connect to someone, or something from a state of alignment, there is a natural flow and exchange of energy that is unlike the heavy, false, insecure connections we often make growing up.

If you are feeling alone right now, like you don't have many people in your life that you can talk to, know that in time you'll continue to shed that which doesn't serve you and call in people you do feel aligned and connected with. At first it may just be one person which is all it takes—if there is one person, or some part of yourself, or even non-human energy in your life that you feel comfortable around, that gets you, focus on that energy and see where it leads. Where we place our focus we allow that to grow. Friends have been invaluable on this journey of mine, and it is one of the leading factors in the title of this book, even if my words are a reminder that you are not alone, that all is as it should be, that I've been there before, well, that in and of itself may be a good start.

A big part of this process is the awareness and trust that you are being guided in the right direction. You may see signs and get nudges from the universe reminding you that you are on the right path, as I will remind you as you read these words that simply finding this book is reminder enough, so I say drop the worrying about whether you are getting this whole awakening thing right or not, release your attachment to what the outcome should look like, and get present to the endless expansiveness and greatness that you are always, your ability to feel all the things, not just the seemingly good ones, sit with that, and see what happens.

Sixteen

On Feeling Alone

I'm an angel, message from God.
I'm an angel, got a message from God.
I'm here to show ya, that we're all the same,
I'm here to tell ya, there's no one to blame.

Cause I'm an angel, message from God.
A free human, do what I want.
I'm here to show ya, that we're all the same,
Here to tell ya, there's no one to blame.

Cause we can fly so high,
You don't have to try.
Just dance the divine,
You'll feel so alive.
Your life is alive.
Your life is alive.
Your life is alive.
Your life is alive.

Maybe someday I'll get it right,
Got the daylight, awake in the night.
I'm a savior for myself.
Do your dirty work, get over yourself.

Cause I'm an angel, message from God.
A free human, do what I want.
I'm here to show ya, that we're all the same,
Here to tell ya, there's no one to blame.
Cause we're all angels.
- Yoshua

Alone:
Having no one else present.

I n the process of breaking free from fear, dissolving the illusion, it's easy to feel alone, to look around at the world we live in, the people we are surrounded by, and feel totally and utterly alone, scared and helpless even. To recognize that you are living in a dream and everyone in it is still asleep, mindlessly playing out their machine conditioned character all while seeing the truth clearly from your perspective, can feel like a terrible curse.

But I'm here to remind you that you are not alone, that this is a natural part of the process, that over time you'll connect more and more to others in the same space, even if one person that gets it, dive into that friendship, it's a gift, a gem from the universe. Don't get caught up on trying to wake other people up, to feel like you need everyone around you to understand, instead explore the connections that do make sense as you start to accept what you must do with all of the ones that don't.

Another piece of this book has been a reminder that I have a gift to spot others that are starting to wake up to the truth of the world we live in, and to connect with them and be somewhat of a guide, as I have intended to do with these words. If you have found this book, please know you are not alone, you are simply one step closer to tuning in to the right frequency. When we listen to a radio that is in between stations it sounds like poison to our ears, the static can drive you crazy, but when we start to turn the knob, dial in to the right vibration, everything starts to get clear and make more sense.

You may be transitioning from a static station to a clear one, maybe you aren't there yet, but you can see it on the horizon, you know it's just within your grasp. Keep tuning in to that frequency, keep connecting to anyone, even if only one other person, that you can relate to, that seems to get it, whether that be a friend, family member, mentor or even an author that you love, let them guide your journey if it feels aligned, always filtering from yourself, not taking things on blind faith. You may one day realize that even the very people that you looked up to aren't where you are anymore, but that's part of trusting the process. Often times people in our lives, friends, lovers, even leaders are no more than a bridge to take us from one side of the spectrum of life to another. But you are your own greatest teacher when you really tune in to yourself.

If you feel alone in all of this, that is okay, I have been there and occasionally slip into that space. But aloneness is a beautiful thing, it is something that every person on the planet shares, no matter how connected everyone looks on the outside, no matter how much you convince yourself that your aloneness is unique, that other people seem to not feel it, we all do, and it is in that shared experience that we are truly not alone. It's one of the great paradoxes of life and when you understand why, you will always be alone in one sense, the feeling of loneliness starts to fade away.

But as I said, you are not alone, and I wrote this book for you, to remind you, to guide you, to allow you to see that once you are on the path to discover truth that it will keep going, that you will naturally leave no stone unturned and the journey will take you to places you can't even imagine, so don't try too hard to make sense of it, or plan for it, just sit back, allow it to happen, and see where it leads you. You can always go back, pretend like none of this happened, slip back into your dream character and continue to play along, but I know all too well that in the back of your mind there will be something else there, beckoning you to continue pushing forward, and even if you jump off the path for some time here and there, it's still the path. Your life is alive.

Seventeen

On Love or Sometɪ.

Love;

*An intense feeling of deep affection. A great interest and plea.
something.*

Affection;

A gentle feeling of fondness or liking.

Fondness;

Affection or liking for someone or something.

Perhaps this is a bonus chapter in a way, or perhaps not. I hadn't planned to write it and I don't imagine it will be all that long, but I have had love on the mind recently, and not so much the "I'm in love" kind of love but more so the "what the heck is love anyway?" kind of love. The first place I turned to was the dictionary, silly I know, to search for meaning to such a vast and ever encompassing word in a dictionary, but I wanted to see what would happen if I started there. Naturally what I came up with above didn't really get me that far, but I suppose it can act as a starting place.

Love, as *an intense feeling of deep affection*, or *to take great interest in something* makes enough sense, I suppose, on one level, but I'm more curious about a few phrases I've been hearing recently from some friends in the mindfulness community, things such as; love is all there is, you have to

Conver

love yourself, and alw...eling
choose love, I can...
sometimes get
on the wall...
Osho ...conceptually
unWhen

...ve over hate. When someone says to ...derstand what they mean, and I even ...eling when hearing it. When I read a quote ...t center I am currently writing these pages in by ...ove is the most healing force in the world," I can also ...conceptually what he means, smiling as I continue on with my ...hen John Lennon sang, "All you need is love," I too can grasp what ne was getting at as I sing along with a big grin on my face, but for most of my life when I would think of the word love, I used to find myself getting confused by what "it" really is at its core and wanted to see if I could clear things up for anyone else that might be in a similar situation.

For such a long time I was struggling to make sense of such a BIG word, a word thrown around in the holiest of places as much as the cheesiest of commercials and holiday cards. They can't mean the same thing, can they? How can one word have so many meanings? When I say, "I love you," to a friend or partner, I think I know what I am trying to convey, I get the deep fondness I am trying to express. But when asked to choose love over hate, or to practice self-love, without really knowing what love is, what good is it for me or anyone? Let's see what we can come up with.

Love, like all things, is ultimately a word that humans have crafted to make sense of something that is really beyond words. If we look at the surface of love we can understand it in one way, but like all things in life, it all comes down to one thing—truth. Ah yes, we always end up at truth. But I want to bring something else into the mix, a concept that gets brought up with love so often, but also gets mixed and mashed around that; *God is a loving God.*

The very idea that God, whatever you may think (or have been told) God to be, is an all loving God, sounds sweet enough. God watches over us, protects us, gives us love and light and healing and all of our hopes and desires. But God, not as a singular being, but as that which makes up the fibers of the entire world, is so much more than that, which for a lot of people actually seems to be a pretty big problem.

I can't tell you how many times I have heard people upset, lost, and confused, feeling justified in not believing in a higher power by hopelessly asking how God, an all loving, just, and fair God, could allow for such hate, violence, and fear in the world. I get the sentiment, but the direction is way off. I keep going back to the same thing, when you ask a question based on an assumption of the question, you'll never have an answer that can truly satisfy you. Destroy the question, unravel your assumed truths until you end up with something you know to be real.

To assume that God is just, or fair, or all loving might sound nice, but what good does it really do? That is why in destroying the question, examining the reality that you assume God has to be a certain way, that you can get to the truth of what God, as well as love, is. Love simply is, just as God is. God, or the universe, or higher power, or whatever label you put on it, isn't some elevated human with magical powers sitting up in some higher place looking down and judging us, but rather in the fabric of our entire being, the genetic, energetic, and spiritual makeup of all that we are.

That is why you hear so often people saying that God is everywhere, God is all around us, God is in everything. You may think God should be a just God, but God is all, so the experience of God, or whatever you call it, comes with all of the bad, just as the good, even though both of those things are ultimately more labels and judgments themselves. The hate, the violence, the love and the war, if you believe in a higher being, you miss the whole point if you don't realize that that being is ALL, not some, not just the good stuff that you like, not only when you need them, but ALL OF THE TIME, ALWAYS, INFINITE.

And on top of that, if GOD is all, you are all, and thus you are one with GOD. You are love, you are hate, you are war, you are flowers, you are all, you are consciousness and at one with every single experience and possibility that could ever exist to infinity and beyond. If you are here for spiritual growth, if you want to transcend space and time, be ONE WITH IT ALL, if you really want to BE HERE NOW, I'd reckon you best start seeing just how much NOW and ALL really is.

I know how it can feel, a heck of a responsibility, to realize that you are capable of anything and that you have the totality of the universe inside of you, not an easy pill to swallow, it can feel like a lot of pressure and responsibility, and maybe it feels best to see God as something outside of you as a way to not have to take on such a profound truth, freeing yourself of all that responsibility. But heck, what's your other option, staying asleep, avoiding life? You choose.

I'd like to think back on the Matrix right now, when Neo, at the very end of the first movie, finally realizes what he is capable of. Throughout the film, the viewer, as well as all of the characters, are on an adventure to discover whether Neo is really the chosen one, whether he can really do all of the things that the prophecies spoke of. Some characters, like Morpheus, believe him to be the one, have full and unwavering certainty, while others question along the way, including Neo himself. We, the viewers, are brought along through the action adventure, trying to decide for ourselves what is true, even if we secretly know that he must be the one otherwise there would likely not be a movie being made for us to watch in such high regard. When Neo does finally realize that he is the one and Morpheus's hopes are confirmed, everything changes and it all comes into alignment.

But what is interesting to me about the whole thing isn't so much that Neo turns out to be the one, but that anyone else in the Matrix doesn't realize they too are THE ONE. Of course, when it comes to movies, I would expect nothing less, but what is it about his awakening to his destiny that allows him to step into his true gifts and powers? If Morpheus had been told the prophecy and decided it was about someone else, would they not have become "the one" instead?

The Matrix represents the false world, and even though Neo woke up to see the truth, he was still caught in another false world, which in some ways can be even more dangerous. I think Neo woke up in the dream, but has he awakened from the dream completely, or is he still caught in another dream, in a world that seems more real than the other one, assuming that it MUST be the real one, which in some ways can be a bigger trap. It's like being asleep, then waking up, and being so clear that what was then false is now real, only to blind yourself to the fact that the world you woke up to may also be another false world to bust through.

It is in this way that I see love. To awaken within the dream we are living in, to recognize that we have been playing a character amongst characters, may be the first step on the pursuit of truth, however, it's not unlike realizing that love is all. "Love" is still just a word with meaning, with assumptions, with conditioned ideas, and when we cling too tight to it, while it may make us feel good, we may still be missing the point, just like folks often do when they assume "God is a just God". I'm not here to knock on love, I freaking love love, it feels good, it's THE word of words. If I was only allowed to say one word, in any tone or form of expression, for the rest of my life, it would likely be "love". But it's still just a word, and as we spoke about at the beginning of this book, words are made up, and because of that, not always the best way to communicate, especially when everyone you speak to has their own definition of the word and will take it to mean whatever they please.

So, if you've been burned by love, or you've been left confused, look at the word, use it as YOUR word to dissect your life, to break down the fabric of existence, and see what's left. If it is really the case that, "all you need is love," while we can see love as being kind, or opening our hearts, or doing the right thing, we are often still limited by such a limitless word. But when love really is all, if we know that consciousness and truth are all, then love is either the same thing, or the love we are experiencing is the false love, the conditioned love. So choose love, or be love, or see love in everything, and know that the love you speak of is beyond what any definition could ever capture, it is at the very fibre of every inch of existence in the universe.

Love,
Your friend Yoshua.

Eighteen

On The End

Have I been lying to you the whole time? Or, is this really just you talking? I've even been in the mindset, on many occasions, where I thought that I had to change, had to mold in to someone specific, someone different, to feel loved and accepted. The more awareness I bring into the false reality of myself, the more I've been coming to terms with the karmic patterns of doubt that have led me to make choices that many might consider poor, even if in the moment it felt like the "right" thing to do. You see, deep down I might be desperate for love, but on the surface of it all, I am a liar. Why do I lie? Because I don't know my own truth.

I've spent over a decade unweaving the cloth of my birthed mark on this existence. Diving into who I am, where my ego comes from, why I make the choices I make, all for the sake, at least I hope, to "better" myself. How can you know that you are lying if you haven't got a clue what the heck you are? When fear kicks in, instead of saying what I am really thinking, I say a manipulated, manufactured version of what I think I should say in that moment. And thus begins the seemingly infinite cycle of watered down, double distilled, bullshit spewing out of my mouth.

While it seems that there are a lot of people out there, others capable of speaking directly from their heart, or at least from their emotional heart, whether right or wrong, I try and filter what is coming through. And why? Because I am afraid of what might happen if I speak my truth, and in most cases it has become automatic. At times I am scared. To be honest, I feel the layer of delusion washing over me, I feel myself making up a story about how the person on the receiving end would react if I was truly honest, and I hide. *Sure, I've grown this part of myself in a big way, but growth is relative, and growth feels good until it becomes the norm and I am beckoned to expand yet again. There is the unaware side of myself, the autopilot responder that thinks whatever bullshit it is spewing is of some real nature, but my heart is so shut down and wrenched of fear that I don't even realize I am lying.*

And all over, through and through, I also recognize that none of what I am sharing really matters, that that too is a story, another layer of judgment that I have picked up to try and convince myself I should know better. "You only ever see things from your perspective!"shouts the frustrated partner, in a desperate plea to get some compassion and empathy. "Well YOU only ever see things from YOUR perspective!", the other partner quickly quips back.

So what is the key to unlocking this great mystery of speaking my truth? What is it that will allow me to find my fullest potential? I am not always lying, at least not in the way that you might be used to—"I'm just out with my buddies, nothing inappropriate is going on, I swear," no, I'm not talking about that kind of lying so much. Not even the "do these pants make me look fat," kind of lying, or the "sorry we can't make it tonight, I'm not feeling well" sort of lying. It's ultimately a much more elusive lie. And that is where we get back to this concept and a freeing piece of the puzzle I like to call "discovering your karmic ancestral debt".

Let me explain;

Ultimately we are born of something, born of an idea, a thought, a feeling, whatever it may be. As a child we come into this world seemingly a blank slate, basic, pure, curious. Ah yes, curiosity, that which, in many ways, truly makes a child a child. The ability to say, "but why?" only to say, "but why?" again, until the parent simply can't go any further. "Dad, why do people drink alcohol?" "Well son, it's a fun thing that people like to do at parties," but why? The son replies. "Because parties are a thing that people like to attend, and drinking makes the parties more fun for them," "but why," the son replies. And so on and so forth...

Curiosity, a most curious of curious things...

Now seems like a good time to step back and dive into the definition.

Curiosity:
A strong desire to know or learn something.

So, as a child in a child's mind we seem to have a built in desire to want to know things, to learn things, to experience everything around us. If we didn't have this innate drive how would we grow and expand? How would we possibly have a drive to learn language, to learn how to walk, to learn how to live, to paint, to swim, whatever it may be?

And it is that innate drive that can ultimately lead us to our karmic pattern of doubt. By studying who we are, by really getting curious about what makes us us, by asking why to everything until there is simply no more why, we can start to unravel the thread that so barely holds us up. But it isn't only with us that the studying, exploring, and researching happens, it is with our parents, our families, both alive and passed on, our friends, and our partners.

The more we see and seek truth within our lives, the more we understand our place in the world. By dissecting our beingness through our curiosities, we begin to break down the lies, fears, and the falsehoods that we believe to be us. It is easy to assume that the tools, guidance, lessons, and morals that we picked along the way are there to protect and serve us, and in many ways that may very well be true in the right context. But it is in our weakest and most vulnerable moments, when the veil of illusion has come crashing down, that we can catch a glimpse of who we are beyond our conditioned habits.

"The unexamined life is not worth living" - Socrates

It's easy to get caught up in a character, even if we secretly know deep down something isn't right in the external, we see other people living out their lives. They seem to really be buying into who they are, confidence radiates off of them, as if they are so sure of themselves, making us, in our imagined comparison, only feel smaller, more disconnected and alone. It can really make us question who the heck we are.

Who am I? The ageless question. The question that the greatest thinkers and wise people have discussed, debated, and even fought over since the beginning of man. And yet it is only through believing that we have a self, believing that we are a singular being in a vast world of differences, that we suffer and get caught along the way. By asking ourselves, "Who am I?", and searching for a satisfactory answer, we are only yet again pulled into the trap of being human, of trying to explain something in words when we know all too well that words, and thus their meaning, however you string them, are all made up. If one day you wake up to find that you've been going the wrong direction the whole time, or if you've been on this path of seeking truth but feeling stuck, perhaps it's time to stop looking for the reasons and look for the only REASON.

There are a lot of people out there living in the "false" world, completely unaware that they are in it, trying desperately to make sense of it all. Funny enough, while there are some who struggle with it and try to come to terms with what is really going on, others seemingly thrive in such a space. There are those that are so convinced and convincing, so incredibly good at playing their role, that you'd almost be fooled, tricked into thinking that what they have to say is in fact real and based in truth. In the context of a lie, any truth can be real.

You can build a vacuum, one where there is a hierarchy, where some people know things and others don't, and within that, yes, there are facts and answers, just like when taking a math test, 1+1 = 2. But it is only in this construct, that is ultimately built on assumptions, built on the human perspective, that we can have what one might be called a fact.

And that is the funny thing about writing a book about speaking your perspective. The moment you write something you either hold on to it, feeling like you need to now believe it, especially if you are going to sell it for others to buy in to and act as though you are being who you say you are. Or you can let that go, hold on as long as you'd like, in fact squeeze it awful tight, and then let it the fuck go. Drop it. Sit back, realize you are doing your best, growing, changing, expanding, and that getting frustrated at yourself for making a mistake, for "failing," doesn't help the situation. Life is changing—the moment you think something, do something, share something, it is no longer yours, let it go, don't get too caught up on what others might make it mean, don't give yourself so much credit.

And so if you lie, so be it! You were told lies your whole life, your parents were told the same lies and their parents were too. How could you have known? You aren't responsible for what you have become, but you can take responsibility for where you will go, and what you will do with it. I am not afraid of fear, I appreciate fear. Fear isn't designed to crush us and keep us small, but rather to show us how big we can really be. One of the hardest things for humans to do is to really dive into the big and scary things in life, going into them means that they might consume us, that we might actually have to take a look, not avoid, and reckon with reality. But that is the beauty of life, there is nothing to be afraid of but fear itself, and fear is only a test to show us what is possible.

And if things get messy, so be it. At some point you've got to pick yourself off of your ass, and get back up. Know that you've learned, you tried, you took a risk, a chance, and that now you can grow, now you can take the next step. Labelling something as a failure is an excuse to stay stuck, but seeing it as experience is a way to push forward and to break into a new dimension of truth. I believe in you. And that is because I am you, believing in you is believing in myself. We are all connected to this world, there really is no separation between you and me, him, his, her, them, they or she.

When we get out of our own way, when we look at how we are, who we are, what we have been taught, what we have picked up from those around us to believe, how the cycles and patterns keep repeating themselves, generation after generation, a great clearing starts to open up. You may not feel responsible for who you are, or you might feel the weight of it completely, but you have a choice to break out of that, own what you've become, and get curious so you can change the things that no longer serve you and see what happens when you drop your false character built on fear and allow something much greater to guide you. I can't really tell you what it is like from the other side, but trying it on don't cost a thing (other than potentially your "self"), so why not give it a go?

Nineteen

On Heartbreak

Hmm, to share, or not to share, that could very likely be the question, but seeing as how I am already sharing, here goes, uh, something. Today was a tough day. Today I learned about a lot of things, all necessary things ultimately, things that make me really happy for other people that I currently or have cared about in the past. Today I found out that the first love of my life, my high school girlfriend, is having a child that is due the exact day of my birthday, March 13th, and on a Friday of all days. That didn't hurt, that made me happy and laugh a bit, oh universe you silly puppy. Today, however, was also the day that I learned some news that crushed my heart, ripped this blood pumping organ to shreds, fed it to the dogs that then shat it out only to then be run over by a truck just for good measure. But before we get into that, I should probably share a bit about heartbreak and breakups.

I remember when the first love of my life and I broke up. We were together for three years, went off to separate colleges, said we'd be fine and stay together yet struggled the moment we were away. It only took us a week before we decided to part ways. It was a mutual thing, a sort of knowing what we had to do. It was sad, we were crying, and just as I was about to walk into my room and sulk, I heard music coming from someone's dorm room, went inside, and ended up playing tune's all night, almost forgetting about the break up. It was a great transition, but as soon as the music stopped, the pain set in.

I was depressed, from what I remember, and what my mom told me, for quite some time. The breakup wasn't so bad in the moment, but a few days later when she told me that we needed to take some space, that even though we said we were going to stay friends, that we needed to take some time before we could really build something new (the later which never really happened, understandably). It was great advice, trying to go from lovers to friends overnight was next to impossible and in the end it allowed us the space we needed to move on. Still, it broke my heart, losing a best friend and lover left an emptiness in me for months. I didn't experience heartbreak again until some years later when I moved to NYC.

My partner and I at the time had fallen deeply in love, but when I moved to Brooklyn and she moved to Vermont, things were fading out. Instead of being honest and telling her I wanted to move on, I did the stupid thing I've done many times in the past and passively aggressively found a way to get her to end our relationship—so mature of me let me tell ya. But then when she did end it I was so hurt, I felt sick, terrible. I've since come to realize that my fear of hurting someone, however bad it may seem in my head and heart, isn't worth hiding from because the alternative, what I did, was far worse.

We got back together for a short amount of time until one day she admitted to me that she was having feelings for someone else. Being so stuck in my head and unable to see the truth, it crushed me. I tried to fight for us for a few hours, saying that what we had was too special and that I wasn't going to give up, until finally realizing that this was what I wanted and had to move forward. Still it was crushing to experience such loss as I reflect on all that we once were—I did everything that I could to avoid feeling the pain. Eventually this heartbreak led me to develop a deep appreciation for journaling and it would be the first step to me completely unwinding my life, the catalyst for me to dig deeply into who I was, sitting in my car, writing everything that I believed. I'm not saying that what happened to me wouldn't have happened either way, but I attribute this breakup to the first step to me discovering who, or what, I really was.

Some years later when my best friend and roommate and I got into a relationship briefly, it was messy. I knew it wasn't right, she knew it wasn't right, but I couldn't shake it and I expressed my deep desire to be with her, regardless of how bad I knew it might be for us. Our romance lasted no more than a few weeks, but once it happened I couldn't shake the feeling. I told her I was all in and wanted to be with her, even if I knew deep down it wasn't right, which only made it far worse. No matter what I did to rationalize the situation, I couldn't get over how I felt.

Things got messy, as you might imagine. We stayed roommates for a while—she wanted to stay best friends, I didn't want to hurt her and took what I could get, which turned out to be a miserable mess. Dealing with the heartbreak of losing what almost was I felt imprisoned by my situation. She was going on dates, coming home at night, jumping in my bed to tell me all about her experiences, or waking me up in the middle of the night to have me eat Mac and cheese with her after a bad date. I let this go on—with no blame ultimately for her—for too long.

I do my best, with a bullet in my chest.
I do my best, do my best with a bullet in my chest.
Cause I am on top of the world.
I am not used to fire arms.
He saw his father and he ran away,

He said you're not my problem.
It's all inside your mind.
It's all inside life.

-Lyrics from Yoshua and The Everybody Band, "Bullet in my Chest"

I used to sit in bed, curled up in a ball, depressed, feeling a bullet in my chest—the heartache, the pain, the loss was overwhelming, I could barely breathe. I would wait for her to return from a date, wondering what had happened, making up all sorts of things in my head about what might be, torturing myself, expecting the worst, visualizing it in full detail. I felt trapped, and I honestly saw no way out.

I remember very clearly lying in bed, arms wrapped around my legs that were tucked into my chest, rocking back and forth like a little scared, helpless baby, pleading with the universe. I would say, "Universe, here I am, a broken man, with nothing to give, no drive, no passion for life, and no clear way out. If I am meant to get out of bed, I trust, even if I can't see it, even if this is the worst pain of my life, that you will find a way to break me out of this miserable hell, and if not, so be it." Low and behold, regardless of how long it took, something, almost divine in nature, seemed to awaken me from my darkened slumber.

And then one day a beautiful alien angel walked into my apartment and my prayers were answered—she broke me out of that hell, and as I would come to find I would break her out of hers, as we fell in love and started a new journey, one that went so deep and so fast that I could not have imagined it in my wildest dreams.

First it was love and some incredibly wild adventures around the world, then marriage and a move to Colorado to continue to grow our life. It wasn't an easy marriage, we experienced the deepest and darkest parts of ourselves, triggers, pains, and traumas, but it was unlike anything that I could have imagined in a million years. It felt like we lived many lifetimes together, living as one another's reflective mirror for truth, diving to the depths of our souls, seeing what love could really be.

As much as we cared so deeply for one another and wanted to make it work, ultimately our paths were going in separate directions and now, as I write this, we are getting a divorce, splitting up our possessions, and going our separate ways. Time will certainly tell, however relative it is, of what may become of our connection, perhaps we remain friends from a distance, supporting one another through thought and memory, or maybe we do find a way to shift out of what we were and keep the friendship that we always had. It is not for me to know these things, but I trust the universe is guiding me and what is meant to be always is.

I want to take a moment to express something about relationships, before sharing the hardest part of my experience, that I have come to notice time and time again. Relationships can be challenging as fuck. I am a little reluctant to "put that out into the universe" as I am not trying to manifest or call in more challenging relationships, as though they have to be hard. I believe they can be easy and simple in many ways. But being in a relationship is like having a magic mirror in front of your face that brings up and shows you all of your deepest and darkest fears and triggers. Most of the people that I know who try to navigate relationships get tripped up in one way or another. Trying to share a life with someone that you love is wonderful, but can be very triggering and challenging on a level that is hard to experience when you are on your own. You can't get away from who you are, I mean you can try, you can bury yourself in work, dig for the bottom of the ice cream carton, or distract yourself with hobbies and such. But when you allow the relationship to guide you into something great, when you take what you are seeing and feeling, and actually look into it, relationships can truly change you for the best.

I meet few people who aren't struggling with relationships. Even myself, after going through a big awakening some years before meeting my now ex wife, believed that I was set, believed that my practices in non-duality, non-attachment and all that were actually things that could help me to stay grounded and not get lost in the whole dance of love. But I was wrong, I still had emotional triggers that went far beyond what my mind thought, things buried deep down forcing me to make silly, or fear based, decisions, to stay in a character, and live out a lie.

I had thought all those years ago that I had dissolved the character, dropped the ego, but while that may have been true in my thought mind, my body had a whole different level of attachment to drop, deep repressed trauma and pain that were really my captors.

I share this because I want to make a big distinction that there are, in some ways, two phases of enlightenment or truth realization. I'm not here to say that this is the only way, or that they both can't happen at the same time, but that awakening from our mind may only be one piece of the process and until we awaken from our being, from our body's conditioned fears, we remain jailed in to our pain. I've come to see that even some of the most tuned in, aware people that I know seem to struggle with this side of themselves and I see how it bleeds into their relationships. Relationships can be wonderful, I'm sure they can also be simple, at least once you've really gone through this process, but they will challenge and test you unlike anything else. Any struggles you have in your romantic life, like anything else, you can heal and grow when you stop blaming and start looking deep within. Okay, back to the story.

Jaquy and I had something I could have never even come close to imagining. Looking back it seemed like our coming together was truly a divine experience (even if technically all things are), the way it all happened, the fact that we could have just as easily never met reminds me that life is always in alignment. But sometimes something that seems like it was meant to last forever, sometimes when we say, "I will always love you," what we really mean is in that moment. Just because something is wonderful and perfect at a time, is meant to be, doesn't mean it is necessarily meant to be forever.

I can dive into a relationship, give myself fully, get lost in all of it, only to find that naturally at some point the universe will guide us apart and elsewhere, but that doesn't make the experience any less meaningful. That is why I see the importance of going full in, not out of fear, or worry of heartbreak and loss, but out of trust. Ultimately, in my case, our lives were going in different directions. When we met we fell madly in love, we helped one another really discover who we were, digging deep into our pain and trauma, and then once we saw who we truly were, I realized that we were not meant to be together anymore, even if such a big part of me wanted to continue to fight for us.

I no longer fear heartbreak, but it certainly wasn't always this way, I used to avoid pain like the plague. It wasn't until something happened to me recently that opened me up to this new space. Rather than share any personal details, I will focus on the feeling that I felt, as that is likely to relate much more than the specifics.

As the words pierced my ears, burning terror into my minds eye, my body started to shut down, the pain began to sink in, and I started to feel like I was going to faint. I checked in with my body, took a few deep breaths, and brought myself back to the room. My fears told me to run, but I had to stay put, I wasn't going to do what I used to do.

As she told me what had happened between her and another, I wanted to know anything she was willing to share. I kept asking for more and more details, no matter how painful it felt.

Having all of my fears confirmed, feeling as though what I had tried so hard to be was never enough, that no matter what I did, I was inherently the "problem," left me in a haze. I felt a knife slowly driving directly into my heart, terrorizing my emotions. The pain was almost unbearable, but I sat with it. She checked in to make sure I was okay, and while I expressed that I was not, I said that I wanted to know more, wanted to hear everything, however painful it was.

In the moment, as the pain and fear took over, I nearly lost myself, but the more we spoke, the more I started to see the importance of it all.

I left for the weekend and my heart began to sink even deeper into despair once I had time to process what I had felt, letting my mind race as I imagined what may have been, my worst fears, in vivid detail. I'm not pretending it was easy in any way, as you might imagine, but it was different from heartbreak I've felt in the past. Even when I saw why things hadn't worked, even as I asked for more and more details, even as I felt the slow blade of the knife piercing my heart, I knew it was necessary. I knew it wasn't going to be easy to move on, even if I ultimately made the choice to leave, but instead of running from the pain, I allowed it in, recognized what I was feeling, named it, and I sat with it.

I'd like to say that it was that simple and that I didn't just go to Costco and stuff my face full with mediocre samples of food, but I did, at least for a few moments before realizing what I was doing. The difference is that in the past I would have done anything to avoid this feeling, to run and hide from it, but now I was ready to feel it. I let the feeling in, I sat with all of its destruction and pain, but I knew it was what I needed and in doing so I started to develop a new relationship with pain, loss, and some of my greatest fears. Ah, how good it is to feel anything at all...

A few days ago, right before I publicly posted about all of the transitions I was going through with my life, sexuality and relationship, someone wrote in on a post and said something to the likes of "You are a fag, I hate you more than anyone, I hate a lot of people in this world but I hate you so much more." In the past a comment like this would have probably gotten to me in more ways than one, but this time it was different. I allowed myself to take in the feelings that were coming up, and then I took a deep breath, blew it all out, and felt nothing but peace. I debated responding back to his comment with a question, but ultimately decided to simply say, "How good it is to feel anything at all."

And that is where I am at right now. To experience heartbreak is to experience life, emotion, and all of the incredible things that come with it. I remember lyrics to a song I wrote way back when, "A wiser man once said that love was real, and all the terrible things it makes you feel. I said; I know you know, I know you know, I know you know." This type of romance and love are beautiful things, to experience intimacy and partnership is a great gift, a wonderful teacher and a human blessing, but so is the loss of the things you love the most. When you feel the goodness it's easy to want it to last forever, and who knows, maybe it will to some degree, but it is the loss of what once was, of something that we remember being great, that creates the suffering. I'm reminded of the beauty of that suffering, to let it in, to honor it, to process it, to experience loss and grief, even if rationally it doesn't feel justified in many ways. Once you drop the ego, see your character, and let it go, suddenly it's not about attachment or non-attachment, but about allowing what is to be as it is.

Pain isn't good or bad, it just is. When I run from it, when I try and avoid it, when I cover up who I am to avoid having a hard conversation, I only diminish truth. Good and bad are relative, they are based on opinions, on ideas, as is heartbreak and love. Naturally being in love feels wonderful and having our heart broken feels terrible, but I attach no specific value or meaning to one or the other, I have sat with both feelings, I have come to appreciate the seeming polarities of both experiences and I accept them equally. Am I going to go around looking for heartbreak? Fuck no, but it will never hold me back from experiencing something simply out of the fear of what it may lead to if it doesn't "work out" in the ways I wanted it to. Besides, who do I really think I am pretending like I know how things are "supposed to" work out? Where is the fun in that?

When I don't attach any specific meaning to all of life's experiences I'm free to go all in on life, no fear, no worries, I simply let go, release control, and trust that what comes my way, whether easy or hard in a moment, is exactly what I need. The ego will tell us that emotional pain is bad, that the good feels are good, but it is only a distraction, it's all just as it should be. Don't assume that being awake means you are just floating in ecstasy on some mountain top all the time without a care in the world, being awake is awakening to the truth of all, not some, not most, not just the good parts, but ALL.

How Lovely it is to Feel Anything at All

And so this is where I will leave you. This book is ultimately a guide to help you do some serious digging into your own life. I share personal stories for the sole reason of creating context for which I was able to explore truth and experience freedom from the great illusion of life in the hopes that you might see something within yourself. I made sure to share a wide range of facets of my life, not just the good and clear parts, not only that which is shiny and attractive, I wanted to paint a picture of the whole to remind you that wherever you are at is exactly where you should be at any given moment.

As I said, this book isn't really about "me" even if it's got a lot of "me" in it. Rather it's a tool to help you take a good hard look at yourself and see what you might discover. Pull that string, write down those thoughts, examine them under the incredible powerful microscope that is clear presence and open curiosity, and see what you end up with. Life makes perfect sense to me, it is completely clear in all the ways it should be and not because there is some magical place where I am finally perfection personified, or that I have attained something that only a few ever will, but because I've dropped the whole pursuit of the false altogether and simply reside as I am.

Once you've discovered the truth of who you are, you might feel empty for a while, like life has no meaning, you might even get depressed as I did, but the feeling will fade as you start to realize that an empty glass is a glass that can be filled with whatever you want. You see, that's it, from the start the glass isn't half empty, or half full, the glass is completely full... of crap, and not just our crap, the crap of the world in which we were raised in, and when we pour out all the wretched stuff that has been rotting in the glass for so long, we are left with a clear and clean container with limitless space to fill life up with. Empty out your container, first get clear on who you really are, and then drink from it with whatever you please.

POST-ENDING TO THE
BOOK THINGY

I suppose I could have called this part of the book the epilogue, but after having traveled for the last 24 hours to get home from Peru I'm feeling too tired to let my brain think about whether this is really an epilogue, and so "ending to the book thingy" seems to make way more sense to my tired mind. As I went through making final edits and adjustments in the past few days, I started to see some small gaps and additions that I wanted to add to various sections. In an attempt to add various notes that I hoped to fill in later I realized it would be easier to save a chapter for the end with those additional bits and pieces instead of messing with the flow of the other chapters.

Below you'll find a series of short writings on different pieces of the chapter content with a variety of things; additional explanations and thoughts on some earlier concepts, song lyrics, quotes I enjoy, and little anecdotes that I felt might support some of the overall themes in the book. Some are mere musings, some are brain farts, some might get you to think, others might make you laugh.

It's been an absolute pleasure spending this time with YOU, and though that might sound odd because you are the one reading my words, whenever I write I think of you. I think of you reading these words, I think of you in your life, on your path, discovering and uncovering the different layers of all that you are, as well as all that you are not, and I especially think of you as you uncover who this "you" really is, or rather, is not.

Life's Great Paradox

In case you've found yourself confused by some of the things you've read in this book, I want to remind you again that everything described in this book is paradoxical by nature. Since words are made up, so too are their meanings—the stories that we construct from mixing and matching these words only really hold weight in the land of the ego. All beliefs and ideas and opinions are just that—beliefs, ideas and opinions. No matter how much research or proof someone has, or will and strength to fight for what they believe, we make the meaning, thus constructing a false world around us.

Part of the human condition is our longing for, and desperate craving to create meaning where there is no actual meaning. All good and fun, I enjoy pondering things, philosophizing and theorizing as much as the next lad, but I don't pretend for one second that my take on something is any more valuable or worthwhile than anyone else's, that would be rather silly (even if that is technically just a belief or judgment). I hold no real emotional attachment to the words I express, what fun would that be?

Think about what happens when you try and search for meaning. What is the meaning of life? Who doesn't want to know that, right? But it is in the searching, the asking of the question itself, that keeps us stuck in a loop, for how can the person that creates the question expect an answer to that question outside of our opinion? Examine the question, don't make assumptions, get to the heart of what you are asking and why, and the answer will no longer be necessary.

It reminds me of quantum physics. The one thing that really spooks a lot of scientists, that not many in the field seem to be able to put their finger on, is something they refer to as the Heisenberg Uncertainty Principle, that says there are limits to the degree to which both the position and momentum of a particle can ever be known. This is due to the fact that electrons cannot exhibit both their wave and particle properties at the same time when being observed.

The momentum of an electron is proportional to its velocity, but based on its wave properties, its position is based on its particle position in space. The Heisenberg Uncertainty Principle is a kind of scientific dilemma: the more you know about something's velocity, the less you know about its position. And the more you know about its position, the less you know about its velocity. The significance of this uncertainty is that you can never know exactly where an atom's electrons are, only where they are most likely to be.

This is what scientists say, and baffles the leading minds almost to the point of avoiding it altogether, but to me it is all very obvious. Trying to define an electron is like trying to answer a question such as "what is the meaning of life?". The person trying to capture the electron fails to realize that there is no electron, that their mind is creating the electron, giving it meaning, trying to create some definitive perfect measurement, but it's impossible because it doesn't exist. How can we expect to capture something that is only a construct of our mind? Since we make the meaning, whatever answer we get is made up and thus we are stuck in a loop. We can't define the exact state of an electron because it has no definite state outside of what we believe.

Science wants a clear definition of things, maybe because it knows it can't turn to God for answers, knows that it can't answer the questions like "what is the meaning of life?" and thus Scientists put in their energy to calculations and experiments, assuming that there must be a more defined meaning to things, but it is only an illusion. 2+2=4 is only true in the context of what we have created, the rules that humans have placed upon it to exist that way in a vacuum. But it's still the same consciousness, no matter how you swing it, trying to define something that has no definition outside of our own beliefs will only keep us guessing, keep us chasing our tail. But who knows, maybe that's all some people want to do, maybe it's in the chase that makes life worth living.

And Now For a Little Rant...

I don't usually allow my mind to run off like this for too long, let alone share it, but who am I kidding—I get annoyed and frustrated from time to time, even if I ultimately know better. Sometimes I find it's best to let it out even at the risk of sounding like I am unaware of where it is coming from, or as though I am blaming someone. I could easily judge myself as though these thoughts are small, but again, just judgments. So here goes...

I'm fuggin tired of spirituality, spiritual readings, teachings, practices, and most of all, spiritual people. Sure I've spent enough time around spiritually inclined and defined people to know that many of them are very honest seekers, and oftentimes some of the most pleasant people on the planet doing plenty of good, but I've just about had it! I've sat in their circles, sang their songs, danced their dance, smelled their sage, and it was lovely and all of the things you might imagine it to be. Heck even some of my closest friends on the planet would define themselves as spiritual as I have myself. I've even been the one hosting the circles and enticing others to sing the songs!

But I'm over it, over the whole spiritual facade. It all makes sense from the outside—someone is struggling in life, looking for a better way to live, to feel more gratitude, more love and connection, so naturally the spiritual marketplace is the first and most obvious place where one could, and in many cases should, go to cultivate these things they desire. Spirituality looks nice from the outside and it often feels really good from the inside, but if seen from the wrong perspective it is only another trap, one so elusive, so ingenious that it even appears to be a path beyond the trap, while in reality being the final veil between truth and falsehood, ego and no-self.

I see nothing wrong with going there, perhaps as a tourist, and I have no judgment or problem with stopping along the way for a pit stop, and dipping my toes in the refreshing water of namaste village. But I know good and well not to get caught up in the illusion of it all, thinking these things are any different from anything else—just another costume for ego to fit in, no matter how much more comfortable it feels.

Now, before you experience a potential trigger bomb, intrinsically what I am saying really has nothing to do with spirituality being good or bad, or right or wrong, nor am I suggesting that you should avoid the spiritual world, but what we often think spirituality to be is what must be examined because our assumptions of it can easily be skewed since the word holds a lot of weight. To assume that someone who has a dedicated yoga practice, eats vegan, and never misses a chance to write in their gratitude journal each morning before turning on their phone, has any more truth, love, compassion, or whatever in their being than anyone else, would be very misguided. They might, they very well could, but it also just might be another ruse. Don't judge a book by its cover, don't assume someone that seems spiritual is, and don't assume that someone that does not seem spiritual is not. You don't have to have glazed over eyes, a crystal dangling from your neck, be dressed from head to toe in white cloth and permeated a distinct smell of palo santo to be awake.

And so yes, I am sick and tired of the spiritual marketplace, because most of it is just a way to sell you something that isn't real, just like the music industry turned music into a way to make lots of money, getting further and further away from the source of music and vibration, so too has the spiritual marketplace. If we are taught to believe that buying the right clothing and having the right types of crystals is going to help raise our vibration, we'll keep buying things because we'll keep needing more. Look around, it's everywhere your eyes land; 5 ways to have more gratitude and love in your life, 20 practices to cultivate peace, the very titles of the books already reinforce our beliefs that we are broken and need to be fixed.

I'm not saying anyone is to blame, again a lot of the spiritual community is filled with wonderful, loving, and honestly beautiful people. I don't share this to bash on anyone, rather to open up your mind to the potential distraction that is keeping you stuck in another veil of untruth. Some of the most spiritual experiences I have had, some of the most profound and life changing books I have ever read, and some of the truly enlightened people I have met had seemingly nothing to do with "spirituality" on the outside, which used to confuse me because I was conditioned to believe that they must if they were to get to a certain place in life. But they simply weren't in the paradigm of that illusion, they just were.

Do not get caught in appearances, the clerk working at the drugstore could be every bit as awake, and perhaps more (even if there is no real measurement scale for these kinds of things), then the guru with his thousands of pupils and hundreds of books. Spiritual egoism and spiritual hierarchy are the same when the word "spiritual" is removed. People are people regardless of their costume or their likes and dislikes. All are subject to the same laws of the universe.

You don't have to believe me, you don't have to care, you could even be upset, but all I am asking is for you to take a hard look, question the gurus and self-help books, see if, when filtered through your own lens, their words hold weight, or if they are just another distraction to keep you feeling stuck. Be your own guru, your own healer, your own guide, and then, and only then, will you know what works and what does not.

Who have you learned from that truly is the thing in which you seek? Can a disciple of an enlightened master who has yet to attain their true form share knowledge about truth from the unenlightened perspective? Can they lead you to the place that they have yet to go? Would you let a medical student operate on you, one who has yet to actually do an operation themselves, even though they read and memorized their textbooks and got straight A's on all of their tests? Just because someone is an expert in knowing about how to do something, if they have not yet done it, what good is that for you?

Only you can get to the other side, not by following those that claim to know more than you about how to get there or can talk a big game, listing off all their favorite spiritual teachings and quotes, but by your own accord. Knowledge about an experience is not the experience itself. There is a teacher inside of everyone, inside of everything, but that is for you to see and to do with as you will.

*Is the Human Half Awake or Half Asleep?

This book is a no-self help book for good reason. If you try and help the self, you may get caught building up the ego, giving it more tools to be able to hold on tight, thus continuing on with the cycle of this and that, right and wrong. Be gone oh silly self, for I help you no more!

A Little On Friends

I have a lot of friends, people I truly love and cherish of all walks of life. I've always had close friends but now I no longer get caught up in needing to be someone for my friends, in needing to impress them, to convince them that I am a good friend, or do things to make them see me in that way. If I get along with someone, I may continue to spend time with them, if I don't I probably won't. I don't actively choose who I spend my time and energy with from a place of need, I don't force it, nor do I attach myself to someone that has no interest in me. If the energy is there, if, having released control and said so long to the false me that wanted to please people, there is still a connection to be had, so be it, that connection we will have!

You Don't Know Until You Know

While still in my Brothers Green Eats days, Mike and I got hired to do a branded gig for a very prominent alcohol brand. At the time I was pretty much over alcohol, sure I can enjoy a good beer or a few sips of wine here and there, but I don't enjoy being drunk, and if anything it makes me more uncomfortable and awkward than not so I generally steer clear of it. They were, however, offering us a lot of money and an opportunity to fly down to their processing plant and film a segment with a TV legend. I just so happened to be watching a new show I enjoyed that he was in the day I got the email, so it felt like divine timing, and still, it was a lot of money to do something simple enough and go on an adventure.

Looking back I could judge myself and get down on myself for "selling out" as I did feel in some ways at the time, it really was about the money and I had all kinds of stories about why it was wrong and right bobbling through my head. But as I reflect on the experience it was actually a moment completely unrelated to the gig that made the whole thing worth it, even if just for the story I am about to share.

After the shoot I saw that Fleet Foxes were playing in town, and since Mike and I were big fans, I snagged us two tickets. Even though it was last minute and the tickets were bought just an hour or so before the show, we somehow managed to get really great seats, second row, just to the right of center stage, for practically face value. The show was sold out otherwise so this felt like a big score, and I couldn't wait to see how it all played out.

The concert was at a beautiful venue, an absolutely breathtaking theatre, historic in all the right ways, nostalgic in all the others, large enough at a capacity of 3600 to feel like you were part of something huge, and yet intimate enough to feel like that hugeness was special. When we got in just as the show was starting and the band came on I noticed almost everyone in the audience was sitting. This made me uncomfortable, even though Robin Pecknold's (the lead singer) music was fairly mellow and harmonic, it swung on the edge of being a stand up or sit down show and at the time it seemed like the audience was mostly chasing the later. But for me that was a no go, if music even has the least bit of rhythm in it I can hardly contain myself and so within minutes I was up and dancing.

The first few songs passed, someone yelled out "Robin, tell everyone to stand," which got a few laughs and a simple reply from him of "It's a free country." I started to relax a bit, feeling like at least a few people were standing and that I wasn't disrupting the peace all that much, when suddenly I got a tap on the shoulder from a woman standing behind me.

"All of us in the row back here," she said, gesturing to a group of people, "have decided that you need to sit down."

"You know, you'll have a lot more fun if you dance," I replied, shit grin on my face, unsure if she was really serious or not.

"We paid good money for these seats," she said, getting frustrated. "If we want to enjoy the concert sitting down, that is our right and you need to respect that by sitting down and not blocking our view."

A wave of frustration washed over me as I slowly started to get pissed. *Are you fuggin kidding me? Telling me to sit at a concert when I want to dance? This is bullshit.* I got so mad and uncomfortable that I walked into the isle where I saw a few people dancing. I wanted to be away from the heavy intense energy I felt behind me as soon as possible. I did my best to forget what happened, standing away from my seat, away from my brother even, dancing in the isle, trying to get into the moment, but something didn't quite feel right. I paused, took a few deep breaths, and in a moment a newfound clarity washed over me, I smiled, felt peace, and walked back to my seat.

When the song was over I turned around to address the women. "Listen, I'm gonna be honest," I said. "When you first told me to stop dancing I could hardly believe my ears, I started to get mad, but then it hit me. My life is a blessing, music is the most important thing to me, and while yes I'd love to get to experience this the way I want, things are good, who am I to take something you need away from you? And besides, I have no idea what you are going through right now, for all I know you are having a rough day and just want to watch the show in comfort and peace."

She started to tear up, I struck a chord. "You're right, it's been a really rough day, I am so grateful you shared that. I'll tell you what, when a song comes on that you really like, stand up, dance, do your thing!"

Immediately I felt so much love wash over me as we created an instant bond. Anytime I went to stand up for a song I would look back to sort of confirm it was okay with her, not in a controlling, but a friendly way, and she would smile and give me two big thumbs up, and the rest was history.

At the end of the show I turned around to thank her for her presence and I noticed that her partner she was with had a huge arm cast on that went from his hand to his shoulder, it was fresh as though he had just had a major surgery or injury that day. You never know what someone is going through, and we can get angry and shut people out, or we can go into it with an open heart and mind and see what happens.

GET OUT!

This book is really about one thing—assisting you in the process of getting out of your way. You want to know what it's like to have pure intentions? Don't try and have pure intentions by trying to judge whether what you do is good or bad, dissolve the ego and then anything you do is pure because you are in alignment with all. Not a small self that does things for wants and personal needs, but a no-self that knows.

Meditation? You say I should meditate? Why would I meditate? What good would that do me anymore? Meditation was a great tool, once upon a time, that helped me quiet my mind, slow down, get introspective, and feel a sense of presence. But I am clear now and it serves me no more, nor I it. Once I've hammered the nail in the wall to hang up the painting why would I keep walking around with the hammer? Put the hammer down and move on. You want to know why I no longer meditate? Because I am meditation. It is my general state, not something I do when I need to feel more calm or peaceful, it simply is.

"The Best Part of Waking Up, There's Nothing in Your Cup."

Once you see the false-self for what it is, life doesn't suddenly get easier. As you shed that which is false, a lot of what originally made you "human" naturally starts to make less and less sense. Your vision clears up and you begin to see anew. But the adjustment can feel awkward and it's not uncommon for your ego to try and slip back in and convince you that you made a mistake or got it wrong.

Sometimes, in moments of total clarity, I find myself pondering the point of it all. When I first came to this place, alone, confused and sad in ways yet excited and filled with wonder, I questioned what the point of it all was since I had seen my entire life was false and meaningless. Why continue on if the character I was playing wasn't real and had no purpose? And what's more, now, recognizing that life was pointless, why create a new character, would that not feel even more phony?

Ego, you sneaky little bastard! Funny how the mind can wander and attempt to create more meaning just to continue its cycle of drama and confusion. Once I got over the trick my mind was trying to play on me, I began to recognize the purpose of my entire journey. The mystery of life is what gives it the thrill. I no longer make decisions in the way that I used to, rather I look for patterns and recognize what is obvious and in flow and almost instantly the thing to do is known. It doesn't mean I don't work hard, or never have moments where I try and force, only that I recognize where it is coming from, step aside, and all becomes clear.

I know how I want to feel, what situations, people, and places are in alignment with my being, just as I know what music harmonizes with my ears, but it is all very much on a vibrational level. The way in which that materializes is the great mystery of life, and one of the things that truly gives it all of its wonder and joy, makes the adventure worth taking. Even the things that seem to go against what I desire, even that which may be considered unfavorable, or negative, is no longer the "bad" to my hope of "good" but yet another energetic experience to flow through.

This journey can be as confusing as it is beautiful. Dissolving your false character is only the first step. Once the ego is gone, you can, as I have touched upon earlier, do whatever feels right. You can write a book, you can start a healing business, you can build houses, you can run a marathon, become a chef, or move to the woods and never speak with anyone again. The dissolving of the false-self may be the beginning, but what you do after that is of your own accord, and that is the beauty and mystery of it. It's rare that there is a day that goes by where I am not completely blown away by the perfection of it all.

For as much as this book speaks about dropping the ego and dissolving the false character, once you've gone through the process, you'll still likely have a "costume" of sorts that you wear around as a way to communicate with the world around you. Call it your ego, your personality, or what have you, once you go through the dissolving process and start to integrate back in to everything, at first it may feel like you are just creating a new character.

This part may feel odd and even confusing in ways, but after you've seen the ego for what it is, you no longer have to worry about whether you have one or not—you aren't living in a dualistic world of ego or no ego, but rather of totality, of wholeness, of oneness, where all is as it should be.

Dropping the ego and the false-self can feel like big and scary things, but the price of truth is everything, and when you have that what you are left with is nothing at all—and nothingness is everythingness. Or something like that...

Bibliography

McKenna, Jed. Spiritual Enlightenment, the Damnedest Thing: Book One of The Enlightenment Trilogy. Wisefool Press, 2011.

McKenna, Jed. *Spiritual Warfare.* Wisefool Press, 2010.

Roth, Gabrielle. Connections: The Threads of Intuitive Wisdom. Jeremy P. Tarcher/Penguin, 2004.

Vonnegur, Kurt. Breakfast of Champions. Dell Publishing, 1973.

Wachowski, Lana. *The Matrix.* 1999; Burbank: Warner Bros. Entertainment Inc. DVD.

You try to go to work,
but something seems wrong.
You write a message to yourself,
to get some help so you belong.

And then the moment comes,
sweeps you away from here,
just sit back, relax,
and listen to YOUR song.

When he sings to you,
you don't know which way to try.
Cause when he sings to you,
It's hard to believe that guy.

When the moment comes,
takes you away from here,
you believe in things,
now it's time to make them real.

It's easy to be free.
It's easy to be free.

And then they call you up,
and they ask about your day.
You have stopped going to work,
And all you want to do is play.

You worry about your bills,
you worry about your health,
and you worry about your friends,
but you don't try to work it out.

So just sit right back,
and think to all your truth.
You cannot understand,
if you do not have the proof.

Just take your time,
and give in to all the good.
I believed in things,
and now I am full.

It's easy to be free.
It's easy to be free.

Like me, to be free,
like me, to be free.

It's easy to be free.
It's easy to be free.

-You and The Everybody Band, "Easy To Be Free"

Made in the USA
Monee, IL
30 June 2020